The Education of a Radical

The author in Nicaragua in 1983.

Michael Johns

THE EDUCATION OF A RADICAL

An American Revolutionary in Sandinista Nicaragua

University of Texas Press ⟨⟨∨⟩⟩ *Austin*

Requests for permission to reproduce material from this work should be sent to:
Permissions
University of Texas Press
P.O. Box 7819
Austin, TX 78713-7819
www.utexas.edu/utpress/about/bpermission.html

◎ The paper used in this book meets the minimum requirements of
ANSI/NISO Z39.48-1992 (R1997) (Permanence of Paper).

Library of Congress Cataloging-in-Publication Data
Johns, Michael
The education of a radical : an American revolutionary in Sandinista Nicaragua / by Michael Johns. — 1st ed.
    p.   cm.
ISBN 978-0-292-73788-4 (cloth : alk. paper) — ISBN 978-0-292-74386-1 (paper :
alk. paper)
    1. Johns, Michael, 1958– 2. Nicaragua—History—1979–1990—Biography.
3. Nicaragua—History—Revolution, 1979—Participation, American. 4. Nicaragua—Militia—Biography. 5. Frente Sandinista de Liberación Nacional. 6. Civil
war—Nicaragua—History—20th century. 7. Socialism—Nicaragua—History—
20th century. 8. Americans—Nicaragua—Biography. 9. Revolutionaries—
Nicaragua—Biography. 10. Intellectuals—United States—Biography. I. Title.
    F1528.22.J64A3 2012
    972.8505'3—dc23   2011041455

For my dear friend Pat
and
my nephew Josh

PREFACE

For ten months in 1983 and 1984 I was a would-be revolutionary in Nicaragua. The experience taught me a lesson. As the American writer Bernard DeVoto says, "Realism is the most painful, most difficult, and slowest of human faculties."

After leaving Nicaragua with vague but creeping doubts about the Sandinista revolution, it took me several years to see the revolution for what it was. It took me another twenty years to see myself for who *I* was: to see why I went to Nicaragua and what happened to me while I was there.

Realism came slowly for Sandinistas, too. Sergio Ramírez was one of the revolution's top political leaders and its chief intellectual. In 1991 he wrote an essay for *Granta* magazine explaining why his Sandinistas had just lost the national elections. After admitting that the Sandinistas' "plans for collectivized farming seriously undermined all possibilities of winning" the allegiance of the peasants—who wanted plots of their own—Ramírez blamed the ruinous plans on his noble desire to keep the land from ever "falling back into the greediest hands." He conceded that Nicaragua's counter-revolution had become a civil war in the countryside, but he explained it by saying that the peasantry's "fears had proved stronger than our promises" and thereby split Nicaraguans into "those who understood the revolution, and those who could not be reached by it." The revolution's main failing, he seemed to be saying, was its poor sales job. Even after confessing that he and other Sandinista leaders had "been arrogant and had lost sight of important elements of political reality,"

Ramírez buried the revolution's internal problems beneath his dominant story line: the mauling of a heroic little revolution in Central America by the big bad imperialist beast of the north. Less than a year after losing power, Ramírez was still too close to his revolution to see it realistically.

In fact, it took him several years to gain the distance he needed to see the revolution on its own terms and in its full complexity. It took him several years, in other words, to see that the revolution's compassion often took the form of paternalism, that its lofty goals were supported by dubious reasoning, that its good intentions excused bad policies, that its concentration of power jeopardized its democratic ideals, that its absolute faith in the goodness of its aim justified a number of heavy-handed means to bring it about. In the end, Ramírez broke with what remained of the Sandinistas. He called his memoir of the revolution *Adiós muchachos* (So long, boys).

Gioconda Belli's memoir is called *The Country under My Skin*. Beginning as early as 1984, says the former Sandinista, "the Revolution slowly lost its steam, its spark, its positive energy, to be replaced by an unprincipled, manipulative, and populist mentality . . . we were feeling more and more like spectators to a process that continued to live off its heroic, idealistic image even though, in practice, it was being gutted and turned into an amorphous, arbitrary mess." Belli might have been feeling like a spectator to a wayward revolution, but she did not quite know it: she remained a revolutionary until the Sandinistas were voted out of office.

While Ramírez and Belli tell brave and searching stories from deep inside the revolution, neither tells the story that I want to tell: how the ideal of socialism—a political ideal that requires almost complete moral and intellectual certainty—breaks down under the pressure of realism. It is a story, in other words, about how much truth one can see of a socialist revolution and still believe in it.

I'm no Voltaire, but as a twenty-four-year-old in Nicaragua I was something like Voltaire's Candide—in the sense that I too was "a young metaphysician entirely unschooled in the ways of the world." And like Candide, I needed many countervailing experiences before finally tempering my enthusiasm for Marx's version of Pangloss's theory that every effect has a direct cause in a chain of necessity leading to the best of ends. A grand theory makes life clear and simple. It provides a sense of control and purpose. It gives you an identity. It even charts your course of action. So it's very hard to give up.

And the difficulty with describing how I did give it up is that, like Candide, I had only the faintest idea that I was losing my faith. I fought a fierce mental battle in Nicaragua about the Sandinista revolution, but I fought it almost entirely in the back of my mind. So I describe the battle through a series of incidents that, without my quite knowing it, were chipping away at my political certainty while eroding my self-image as an American revolutionary working for socialism in Nicaragua.

Realism does not mean seeing things as they really are. Truth is elusive, especially in politics. Realism means thinking realistically. At its simplest, thinking realistically means allowing yourself to see what George Orwell called "uncomfortable" facts—uncomfortable because they confound your view of the world and your place in it. That is why DeVoto said realism is painful, difficult, and slow. And it is why someone as smart as Charles Darwin had to force himself to follow what he called, in his autobiography, "a golden rule, namely, that whenever a published fact, a new observation or thought came across me, which was opposed to my general results, to make a memorandum of it without fail and at once; for I had found by experience that such facts and thoughts were far more apt to escape from the memory than favourable ones."

While in Nicaragua, I had none of Orwell's capacity to stare down uncomfortable facts. Nor was I wise or honest enough to follow Darwin's rule of writing down everything that ran counter to my ideas. But I did manage to see, if unwittingly, just enough of the Sandinista revolution to get my first lesson in realism.

The Education of a Radical

O*n October 25, 1983,* I woke up in Managua to the news that the United States was invading Grenada, a tiny Caribbean island whose socialist government was friendly with Cuba, Nicaragua, and the USSR. Like everyone else who heard the news that morning in Nicaragua, I could not help wondering if we were next.

Nicaragua's revolution was led by the Frente Sandinista de Liberación Nacional, which Nicaraguans called either the Frente or the Sandinistas—or, if they hated them, the *comunistas*. Immediately after defeating the longtime dictator Anastasio Somoza in July 1979, the Frente confiscated his sugar estates, coffee farms, cement factories, construction companies, and slaughterhouses. The Frente went on to seize the nation's banks. It then appropriated the properties of rich Nicaraguans living in Miami. It even took over the import-export business.

All at once the Frente found itself with a huge piece of the national economy and, as its leaders liked to say, "the guns in our hands and the people on our side." And so it launched its revolutionary program of transferring the nation's wealth and power to itself—as a self-appointed vanguard in charge of leading the people to what its visionaries called a "new society."

By the time I arrived in early June 1983, the Frente's revolutionary program was under attack from *contrarevolucionarios* who were backed by the American government. The *contras* raided Sandinista co-ops and collective farms along the border with Honduras. Late that summer, they briefly took over a Nicaraguan town on the border with Costa Rica. They even tried bombing the military airfield at Managua's Sandino International Airport, though the pilots missed their target and crashed into the passenger terminal. Just ten days before the American invasion of Grenada, contras used speedboats supplied by the CIA to fire on and explode fuel tanks in Nicaragua's port of Corinto, whose twenty thousand inhabitants had to be evacuated.

The fighting was far from Managua, where I was living. It was equally far from the capital's two neighboring provinces, where I was doing a study for the Sandinistas. Even so, the daily reports of attacks and killings, along with the Frente's incessant warnings of an impending American invasion, created an atmosphere of danger that encouraged my fantasy of being a revolutionary intellectual. The fantasy was easy to indulge because the possibility of real danger seemed so remote—until I woke that morning to the news of Grenada.

After hearing the news, I went directly to the Center for the Study and Investigation of the Agrarian Reform. I had been working at the Center for three months. I got in by luck, for I went to Nicaragua with nothing but a tourist visa, $1,500 in cash, the name of someone at the Agrarian Reform Ministry, and the idea of being a revolutionary intellectual— an idea that took root some three years earlier.

The idea did not come naturally from my background. I grew up in a neighborhood whose blue-collar families were doing too well to care about politics, never mind left-wing politics. Nor was I searching for a connection to something larger than myself. I had always liked being alone, and I showed an early impatience with spiritual feelings of all kinds by picking Judas for my Catholic confirmation name. I was not instinctively affronted by social inequalities, either. In fact, my sense of injustice was entirely personal. Although I felt sorry for particularly weak, unlovely, or unintelligent individuals and I sometimes stuck up for people who were being picked on or taken advantage of, I never resented the rich, commiserated with the poor, or disliked the authorities. If I had a general belief about the injustices of life when I was twenty, it was probably that people got what they deserved so long as they were accorded fair play.

The idea of being a revolutionary intellectual took hold, instead, in a simple character flaw: wanting to believe that I knew better than everyone else. And it took hold at a perfect moment: I was three years into college and still looking for a course of study and a sense of myself.

Michael Johns

I found the answer on the twenty-five-cent table of a used bookstore in Amherst, Massachusetts. It was *The Social and Political Thought of Karl Marx*, by someone named Shlomo Avineri. The author dedicated entire chapters of his book to subjects wholly unfamiliar to me like consciousness and society, the logic of capitalism, and the proletariat as the universal class. Several sections read like a foreign language that I barely knew. Words like "praxis," "negation," and "dialectics" sent me to the dictionary. Yet it all seemed deep and important somehow. So I read a few more books about Marx and took a class on the political economy of capitalism.

A half year later I saw the world almost entirely through Marx's categories. I saw individuals as embodiments of their places in the "class structure." I saw capitalists making profits off the "surplus value" they took from workers. I saw the "false consciousness" of working-class people who succumbed to the "fetishism of commodities" and believed in the very system that exploited them. I saw how private property and the profit motive "alienated" people from their work, from themselves, from each other. I saw the "unequal exchange" by which Europe and the United States sucked the wealth out of Asia, Africa, and Latin America. I saw the "internal contradictions" of the "accumulation of capital," contradictions that would eventually cause the ultimate crisis of capitalism. At even higher levels of abstraction, I saw the "economic base" of society shaping its "cultural superstructure," and I saw the "forces of production" and the "relations of production" creating the "modes of production" that determined the various stages of human history.

I thought I was seeing nearly everything, when really I saw almost nothing. My meager experience of life gave me little wisdom about it, while my limited study of history, and of my own times, gave me little understanding of either. But the Marxian categories made up for my lack of real knowledge. They gave me a big, coherent, powerful model of the world. They uncovered what seemed to be the inner workings of history. They added up to what Marx called a science of society. And in so doing, they gave me a heady feeling of intellectual control—and they made me feel a lot smarter than I really was: "With Marx," I said to a friend, "you have the whole world by the short and curlies. Who needs anything else? It's all right there in Marx!"

Thinking I had the whole world by the short and curlies made me want to do something about it. Marx's intellectual system, after all, is equally a political ideal. In fact, the entire thing boils down to an intoxicating notion: capitalism causes our problems and socialism can solve them. It is intoxicating because it makes you feel right *and* righteous—by giving you *the* analysis and *the* answer.

While the ideal of socialism was no more than a distant possibility in the United States, it looked like a real and immediate opportunity in Central America, where the Sandinistas had just taken control of Nicaragua and Marxist guerrillas were fighting right-wing governments in El Salvador and Guatemala. So I joined a student group called the Latin American Solidarity Association. We wanted the United States out of Central America and the region's revolutionaries in power.

Our chief activity was sitting at an information table in the student union building. We handed out "fact sheets" on Central America and sold copies of a magazine called the NACLA *Report on the Americas*. Almost everything I knew about the Sandinistas came from an issue of the magazine dedicated entirely to the revolution. I read it three or four times to make sure I had the necessary facts and arguments to promote our line about the Sandinistas, which we borrowed from the magazine. "It is clear," NACLA asserted in 1980,

> that this revolution is for the workers and peasants. It also
> appears that the Sandinista Front is carefully and creatively
> laying the basis for a socialist society, knowing full well that
> the dependent capitalist society inherited from Somoza could
> not be reformed so as to provide any future for the masses. As

*one worker said, "We are a poor country with many problems,
but there can be only one solution for us—socialism." This
was echoed by a rural organizer for the Association of Rural
Workers, who declared that, "Our real enemies are all the
bourgeois elements."*

None of us had any idea what the words "revolution," "socialism," or "bourgeois elements" truly meant, but we liked the feelings of heroism, hope, and danger that they conjured up. Most of us had never been to Latin America, and yet we were absolutely certain that we had taken the right side in what we saw as a colossal struggle between American imperialism and national liberation. And even though our politics were those of the information table in the student union and the editorial page of the college newspaper, we all felt like we were bravely standing up to our government. We cheered loudest when the radical professor who spoke at our student rally against U.S. policies in Central America called us "the conscience of the nation."

In the book *Visions of History*, Mexico historian John Womack says American students go in all innocence to Latin America and get turned inside out by the rank injustice that they find all around them there. That's why, he says, they "come back reds of one kind or another."

I was already a light shade of red before going to Mexico, where I spent several months collecting data for my senior thesis about the central marketplace of a small city in Chiapas. But Womack was right. Crippled beggars in the streets, country kids with distended bellies, Indian women washing their hair in fresh rain puddles, cops openly soliciting bribes, American consumer products displacing Mexican culture—the sight of all that turned me inside out.

What really turned me into a red, however, was becoming friends with a Mexican revolutionary. Maricela had the nervous habit of biting off split ends from her long, black hair. She came from a middle-class family and was studying at the local college, which was nothing more than a cluster of small concrete buildings on the edge of town. She was supposed to be studying economics, but mainly she read Marxism. Her favorite book had the optimistic title *Late Capitalism*. Maricela had so thoroughly annotated and underlined it with her fat multicolored pen—she used red, blue, green, and black in declining order of importance—that from a certain distance the pages looked like Jackson Pollock miniatures.

I had my *Marx-Engels Reader* and held my own with Maricela during discussions of Marx's ideas, but it was clear to me that she was living Marxism while I was merely thinking it. She always insisted, for example, that "there are only two social classes, politically speaking: those for a revolution and those against it." She often complained about the indigenous people in the surrounding hills. They saw themselves as Indians instead of peasants or proletarians, she said, which prevented them from making class alliances with people from outside their villages. When we sat in the central plaza to watch the townspeople, Maricela sneered at shopkeepers she considered petit bourgeois and small-time bureaucrats whose "little minds think trivial thoughts." She had even less respect for the do-nothing Marxists who studied at the local college but stood by while she helped poor peasants take over land that was not theirs. The goal of taking over the land, she said, was to organize the peasants into a larger movement that would overturn Mexican capitalism.

The ferocity of Maricela's convictions intimidated me. Sometimes she even seemed fanatical. But I looked up to her and told myself that her Marxism was more advanced than mine. She backed her ideas with action, after all, and Marxists who combine theory with practice are by definition the best kind of Marxists. Not for nothing did Maricela regularly quote Marx's famous line "Philosophers have only interpreted the world in their various ways; the point, however, is to change it."

Her boyfriend was a skinny chain-smoker who had fled some kind of political trouble in a neighboring province. He even had an alias, which made it impossible not to admire him. One day he showed me how to *romper el enemigo*—break with the enemy—in this case by getting rid of the person tailing him. He and Maricela knew all the alleys in the neighborhoods and every downtown store with a rear exit.

I thought they were exaggerating the danger until Maricela was abducted. Her captors kept her bound and blindfolded for two days, all the while pressuring her to name other comunistas and to quit organizing peasants. Then they dumped her on the edge of town. Maricela was scared but said only that she would have to be more careful from then on. Thirteen years later she was part of the Zapatista uprising in Chiapas.

I returned from Mexico cultivating a small, private fantasy of myself in the famous poster of Che Guevara that Maricela had given me as a farewell gift. The red-starred beret, the thin beard, the sensual face, the shaggy hair, the keen eyes gazing knowingly and boldly into the future: the photographer was right to call his photo *The Heroic Guerrilla*. Like every young radical, I wanted to be like Che.

Although I was no closer to being anything like Che after my first semester of graduate school at the University of Wisconsin, I did now think of myself as a full-on Marxist. And I wanted my professors and fellow students to know it. I even wanted my parents to know it.

So I gave my father a book called *The Twilight of Capitalism* as a Christmas present. My father had native smarts. He could fix anything. And he was a good judge of character. But he only ever read instruction manuals and the *Worcester Telegram and Gazette*. Still, he put on his glasses and sat on the living-room couch with *The Twilight of Capitalism*. He gave up after ten minutes. "Here, you read it," he said. "I can't understand a word."

It was not my intention to embarrass him. I even felt a pang of remorse. But mainly I felt the sense of superiority that compelled me to give him the book in the first place. For I wanted my father to know that I was a really smart guy who had moved on to a bigger life and now understood things about capitalism and imperialism and socialism that he and the rest of the people in our blue-collar neighborhood could not even begin to comprehend.

Luckily for the both of us, I was not strident enough to give him my critically enlightened opinion on the small-town life that had given me a happy boyhood. According to my callow and radicalized brain, all that my parents and their neighbors wanted was a secure job, a faithful spouse, a friendly street, a big television, a lawn without weeds, a kid in a community college, a good season for the Boston Red Sox, a new car in the garage, a used one in the driveway, and Friday night pinochle games with highballs and salted peanuts—perfectly good things that most people would be lucky to have but which my Marxist vocabulary limited me to describing with terms like "alienated," "one-dimensional," and "false consciousness."

During my second semester of graduate school I decided to return to Chiapas to do summer research for my master's thesis. I needed a professor from outside my home department of geography to serve on my thesis committee. So I went to see a sociology professor who studied economic development in Latin America.

He impressed me at once by coolly motioning for me to come in and sit down while he finished a phone call in Spanish. "Some comrades in Central America," he said with a smile after hanging up. His loafers, slacks, and sports jacket made him look conventional, but I knew from fellow graduate students that he was a Marxist who spoke out against U.S. policies in Latin America and had done research for the Sandinistas. His thinning gray hair and deep crow's feet made him look older than my father, who was also in his late forties. I chalked it up to the professor's reputation for hard living and political daring, which, according to the rumors, had earned him the respect of left-wing intellectuals in several Latin American countries.

Before telling him my plans for summer research, I wanted him to know that I too was a Marxist. So I mentioned the key names in the academic literature that provided the scholarly trappings for my research. He nodded sympathetically when I complained that none of the professors in my department really knew Marxism. We both laughed when I told him that my main advisor would only tolerate what he called a "Marxist sandwich," three thick chapters of objective meat bounded by two thin heels of Marxist bread.

The sociology professor then listened to my plans for conducting a class analysis of the central market in the small city of San Cristóbal in Chiapas. I wanted to build upon my senior thesis about two wholesalers who controlled the market's three hundred retailers and monopolized the buying of produce from thousands of Indian peasants in a dozen surrounding villages. The professor asked some questions about my study, but mainly he seemed interested in the fact that I had done several months of fieldwork as an undergraduate.

As soon as we finished talking about Chiapas, he surprised me by asking my opinion of the Sandinistas. He cut me off after a minute and said, "Look, why don't you drop Mexico and go instead to Nicaragua? Politically speaking, Nicaragua is the most exciting place on the planet. You would have a chance to do research that really matters. Your project in Mexico is all set up, I know. And it looks interesting too. But it won't mean anything politically. Working in Nicaragua would. I don't have to tell you that Nicaragua may be your only chance to work with a revolution."

Chiapas was beautiful. Maricela would be there. And after eight or ten weeks, I would have plenty of material for a good master's thesis. So it took me a moment to adjust to the idea of giving up a sure thing in Mexico for the possibility of working for a revolution in Nicaragua.

The idea became increasingly attractive as the professor related the thrill of taking Marxism off campus and doing politically engaged research for a revolutionary movement that was looking to build a new model of Third World socialism. All at once I felt terribly excited about the prospect of working in Nicaragua. I even felt guilty for not having thought of it on my own. But I also felt the prod of fear—the fear of being a hypocrite and a coward were I not to go.

The professor said he knew someone at the Agrarian Reform Ministry and would make a call. "The ministry needs good researchers," he said. "And as you well know, a thoroughgoing agrarian reform is key to the success of any revolution in a peasant country."

When he saw that I might just do it, he issued a dose of reality that seemed like a dare—and I had always been susceptible to dares. He warned me that his contact might be of no help. He explained how hard it was for outsiders to get work inside the revolution. Even with luck, he said, it will take a couple of months to get invited to work on a project in the ministry.

Only then did it occur to me that we were not talking about summer research. We were talking about many months, perhaps years. The professor then called my bluff, as it were: "But you look like you can handle yourself; I think you'll be able to figure it out and make a real contribution to the revolution."

I had never been to Nicaragua. I didn't know a single Nicaraguan. I had not even dreamt as a boy, after reading about Nicaragua's famous sea turtles, of seeing them for myself. But all of a sudden I felt a compelling if entirely abstract connection to the place: its leaders were revolutionaries, their revolution was socialist, and working for them would make me a revolutionary rather than a merely academic Marxist.

3

The Center for the Study and Investigation of the Agrarian Reform occupied a confiscated house in an upscale suburb of Managua. The Center employed some two dozen people, most of whom were only a few years older than I. They studied farming and ranching, which employed 70 percent of the country's workers and accounted for 80 percent of its exports, and they investigated the Frente's agrarian reform, which was supposed to turn Nicaragua's backward countryside to modern socialist agriculture.

A colleague later told me that I was the only person ever to walk in off the streets and get a desk at the Center. If that was true, it was true only because Sergio and Osvaldo were the first persons I met there. We took an instant liking to each other. And they seemed to respect me for going to Nicaragua with no grant money and nothing arranged: my professor's contact was useless. They especially appreciated my willingness to do whatever kind of research the Frente wanted me to do.

For three or four weeks I sat in the Center's conference room reading reports and studies brought to me by my two new friends. Sometimes we ate lunch together. Once or twice we drank beer. Then we saw Luis Buñuel's *The Discreet Charm of the Bourgeoisie* when it played at Managua's art-house cinema. We enjoyed watching Buñuel strip away the bourgeoisie's coat of calm respectability to reveal its core of anxious hypocrisy. A day or two later, Sergio offered me an empty desk in the office he shared with Osvaldo. He had somehow persuaded the Center's director to let me hang around.

I was too excited about the revolution to wonder what giving a desk to someone as young and inexperienced as I was said about the caliber of the Sandinista intelligentsia. And I was too beguiled by my suddenly improved chances of becoming a revolutionary intellectual to see my situation in anything but the most romantic terms—especially when Osvaldo, who looked like a skinny version of a young and tanned William Holden, gave me a gift of Karl Marx's *Manifiesto comunista*. It was the last copy, he said, from a boxful he smuggled in from Costa Rica during the last year of Somoza's dictatorship. On the inside cover of his gift he wrote, "To an American revolutionary."

Osvaldo's inscription humbled and flattered me. I had just gotten a desk, after all, with Marxist intellectuals who not only enjoyed the backing of a revolutionary government but had done things that I could only envy, admire, and wish I had been a part of. The assistant librarian, for example, was badly wounded fighting Somoza's National Guard. Almost everyone else had fought in some way against the dictator. Two South Americans escaped the persecution of right-wing military regimes in their own countries before coming to Nicaragua to work with the Frente. An American doctoral student had been at the Center for two years already. And the Center's director was one of the Frente's top intellectuals. According to Sergio, he answered only to the nine *comandantes* who ran the revolution.

Naturally I was anxious to live up to Osvaldo's inscription. My chance came a few weeks later. On behalf of the director, Osvaldo invited me to do a study of the coffee and cotton harvests in the nearby provinces of Carazo and Masaya. The Agrarian Reform Ministry wanted to know how many people harvested the crops, where they came from, whether they had any land of their own, and what other kinds of work they did.

The study would take half a year, Osvaldo told me, and it would mean spending most of my days in Carazo and Masaya. I would be working alone and without pay: they needed to see my work before offering me a full-time job. Osvaldo told me to think about it. Something better might come along, he said. When I leaped out of my chair all ready to go, Osvaldo laughed and said I didn't have to start until the next day.

That evening I copied onto the inside cover of my pristine field notebook a line from a speech that one of the comandantes had given to the Association of Nicaraguan Social Scientists—"Your maxim must be: Social science in the service of the Revolution—in practice as well as in theory."

For the next three months, I made the comandante's maxim my own. I even saw myself as the American revolutionary that Osvaldo said I was. Then I woke to the news of U.S. troops invading Grenada.

4

From fifty or sixty yards away, I saw a dozen people standing in front of the Center. I couldn't tell what they were doing until I got close enough to see that two or three of them had shovels. The men in the group were taking turns digging what would become a long, narrow, chest-deep trench from which to fight the Americans in the event of an attack. The librarian and two secretaries were not prepared to shovel in their skirts and heels, but they were too nervous to stay inside and work.

They all seemed to notice me at once. They stopped talking and watched me come toward them. As soon as I got close enough to say hello, one of the shovelers stepped out of the ankle-deep trench. I immediately took his shovel and started digging.

I did not decide to dig. I didn't say to myself, "Man, I hope the Marines don't come here, but if they do I'm ready to fight for this revolution." I simply took the shovel and started digging. It seemed like the only thing to do. In reality, I had no choice. Not digging would have demonstrated indecision, a lack of commitment, perhaps even cowardice—hardly the stuff of the American revolutionary that I wanted to be. Not digging surely would have cost me the respect of at least some of my colleagues. It might have even cost me my desk. And losing my desk would have compelled me to leave Nicaragua.

I didn't think those thoughts, but I did have a certain awareness that this was a big moment for me, even a test of sorts. So I took the shovel, started digging, and tried to act as though I was merely doing what any other supporter of the revolution would do.

But I was no ordinary supporter. I was a gringo. And digging a trench is not the same as fighting from one. By grabbing the shovel, however, and digging like it was a perfectly natural thing to do, I was saying, in effect, that I was ready to defend Nicaragua's revolution against American soldiers. My colleagues seemed to believe it, perhaps because defending the revolution was for them the only thing to do. I seemed to believe it too—but only because I didn't let myself think about it.

Nobody said a word during my first minute of digging. I could feel the unease behind the silence. A secretary then came running out with a pair of gloves she got from the janitor. She tried to give them to me. "Thanks," I said, "but I don't need them." "Please Miguel," she said, holding them out for me and probably thinking that I was too shy or polite to be the first to wear them. "Go ahead and put them on." "No thanks," I said. "I really don't need them."

I wasn't too shy or polite to be the first to wear gloves. I wasn't even trying to look tough. I was simply displaying an attitude that had become ingrained during teenage summers of baling hay and digging post holes on a dairy farm, where only sissies wore gloves.

"You don't need gloves?" she asked sarcastically. "Don't be an idiot, Miguel. Put them on. You're acting more macho than a Nicaraguan!" After an awkward pause, everyone laughed. I took the gloves and made a show of putting them on. Osvaldo patted me on the back. "Only gringo revolutionaries wear gloves!" Sergio cried. The secretary then smiled and said, "I didn't really think you were a macho, Miguel." The tension was gone. We were on the same side.

I took my turns shoveling. I even took part in the nervous speculation about an invasion. But I never stopped to consider my situation. And my colleagues were too polite, too credulous, or too absorbed in their own thoughts to ask if I was really willing to fight from the trench that I was helping them dig. At that moment I would have said yes, and I would have meant it. Just hearing the question, however, might have given me pause, for it would have been the dose of reality that I was afraid to give myself.

The director came outside around noon. He was in his early thirties. He had a slight build and quivery green eyes. He wore jeans, a jersey, and army boots, the uniform of the Sandinista intellectual.

Everyone at the Center had read his major essay, "The Third Social Force in National Liberation Movements." Because Nicaragua had a tiny industrial proletariat and a large but conservative peasantry, the Frente had to recalibrate the standard Marxian formula for building socialism. To that end, the director identified a third social force made up of youth, students, and the alienated middle sectors of the towns and cities. Under the guidance of the Frente's vanguard revolutionaries, this third force would become a substitute working class that, according to the director, would fight against the capitalist order and in favor of a new society. Like everyone else at the Center, I believed in those ideas—and in the director for coming up with them.

Until that day the director had never spoken to me. I considered myself lucky to get a nod when he stuck his head in the office looking for Sergio. So I was surprised when he came over to me and guided me by the elbow to a spot some thirty or forty feet from everyone else.

"What's your line on the intentions of American imperialism?" he asked. A revolutionary intellectual is supposed to have a line on everything, and I had formed mine after three hours of shoveling and talking about the chances of Reagan invading Nicaragua. But my line was more of a hope than a thought.

"Nicaragua isn't Grenada," I said confidently. "The Sandinista revolution is too popular, its army too strong, and its leadership too unified for an American invasion to result in anything other than a protracted war with no chance of victory for either side. An American invasion of Nicaragua will only produce a small-scale Vietnam. And nothing," I assured the director, "scares an American president more than the thought of another Vietnam."

He looked skeptical. Like most of my colleagues, the director thought the United States was going to invade any day now. The attack on Grenada had rattled even the level-headed Sergio, who had been saying all morning that Reagan was going to "ride his cowboy imperialism right into Nicaragua."

But I stuck to my line. And in my desire to convince myself that it was true and to impress the director with my knowledge of American politics, I went too far. "What will ultimately prevent Reagan from invading Nicaragua," I said, "is his fear that millions of Americans will take immediately to the streets."

"Just like the millions of Americans," asked the director, "who are taking to the streets right now over their government's criminal invasion of Grenada?" He smiled forgivingly, patted me on the arm, and walked to a waiting jeep that took him, we later learned, to an emergency meeting with the comandantes.

I had just made a fool of myself, but I knew that the director had taken me aside to show everyone that I belonged. As I walked back to the welcoming eyes of my comrades, I truly felt as though I had taken the side of a revolution that my government was about to attack.

We stopped digging in the middle of the afternoon and took a ministry bus to a rally at the Plaza of the Revolution, formerly the Plaza of the Republic. The new name was appropriate; the Sandinistas wanted to replace the idea of a republic with their ideal of a revolution.

But the new name did nothing for the plaza itself, a shattered relic in the empty space that used to be downtown. The city center had been flattened by an earthquake ten years before. Nothing had been rebuilt. Little had been repaired. Trees had not been planted. Only here and there did a functioning building stand out amid block after block of vacant lots, piles of rubble and rubbish, and the scattered frames of ruined structures that served as makeshift dwellings enclosed by sheets of tin, tarpaulin, and heavy plastic. The obliterated downtown reminded me of a Dalí landscape: exposed, desolate, and lost to time in the blistering heat.

We were in the plaza only because the cathedral was still standing. Its windows and roof were gone, its walls fractured, its contents removed, and its doors shuttered. But there it stood, a three-tiered, two-steepled, neoclassical pile built of concrete on a metal frame in the 1930s. And there we stood too—because a huge portrait of Augusto César Sandino was hanging from its portico.

Sandino had been the official symbol of the Frente Sandinista since its founding in the early 1960s. Now he was the patron saint of the revolution. And he was everywhere. Sandino typically appeared as a silhouette—of either a small man in a ten-gallon hat or a shadowy face peering out from the brim of a Stetson. His image was usually two or three feet tall and stenciled on walls, doors, and fences, with smaller replicas on trees, stop signs, and telephone poles. From a passing car or bus you saw more hat than man. A friend of a friend, who knew nothing about the revolution but had flown to Nicaragua to start a trip to South America, got out of his cab from the airport and asked, "What's with all the hats?"

To all of us in the plaza that afternoon, however, the image of Sandino provided the perfect backdrop to the speaker who was berating the American imperialists from the steps of the cathedral. Unlike my friend's friend, we never mistook Sandino for a hat. We didn't even see him as a man. We saw him instead as the incarnation of national sovereignty and anti-imperialism.

Sandino acquired the status of a symbol by fighting a guerrilla war against U.S. Marines from 1927 to 1932. The United States had been keeping a small number of troops in Nicaragua almost continuously since 1909, and it did not hesitate to use them as leverage to broker deals in favor of the most pliable among Nicaragua's inept and perpetually feuding leaders. In 1927 Sandino entered the treacherous world of Nicaraguan politics by recruiting a band of soldiers to take a side in the latest round of factional fighting. The Americans eventually stepped in to arrange a deal that was unfair to Sandino's faction but accepted by all the other players. He fled to the hills, infuriated by the other side for winning, by his own side for giving in, and by the Americans for imposing a settlement.

Sandino vowed to fight until his side gained the presidency. Only months later did he turn his anger about the deal into the larger cause of national sovereignty. This time he vowed to fight until the Americans left Nicaragua. And he did. What several companies of Marines could not do in five years of sporadic mountain warfare, however, the head of Nicaragua's new National Guard did by treachery in one night in Managua. Anastasio Somoza's henchmen murdered an unarmed Sandino after he left a dinner party at the house of Nicaragua's new president.

Sandino was the perfect symbol for the Frente. His Army in Defense of the National Sovereignty fought long and hard to drive the Americans from Nicaragua. He sided with the peasants and the workers but never declared himself a communist. He said pithy things that became Sandinista slogans, like "A Free Country or Death," "Only the peasants and workers go all the way," and "The sovereignty of a people is not discussed: it is defended with a rifle in hand." As if all of that were not enough to assure his political deification, Sandino died a martyr at the hands of the villain who built the family dictatorship that would rule Nicaragua for nearly a half century.

So it's no wonder that the Frente plastered the country with Sandino's image, barred anyone else from using Sandino for political purposes, and spread a simple message about him through its newspaper, its radio and television stations, and the schools. The message was this: Sandino was a true patriot, a friend of the poor, and the great and principled defender of Nicaragua's sovereignty.

For its more sophisticated supporters, the Frente produced books like *The Basic Documents of Sandinismo* to deliver the same message in a different language. *The Basic Documents* gave intellectuals like Sergio and Osvaldo their image of Sandino as a nationalist, an anti-imperialist, and a proto-socialist. It did so through a careful selection of his letters, of the favorable press coverage of his rebellion, and of a set of essays written in the early 1960s by the Frente's founder, Carlos Fonseca, who wrote the essays to explain the meaning of Sandino to the first generation of Sandinista cadres.

I read *The Basic Documents* in Nicaragua and accepted the Frente's line about Sandino and his rebellion. I saw the many thousands of silhouetted Sandinos and thought they expressed the revolution's cheeky and playful charm. And I admired the real Sandino for fighting the American occupiers.

But I never identified with him as either a revolutionary symbol or a historical figure. I was not Nicaraguan, so I felt no patriotic attachment to Sandino. I was not in the Frente, either, so I had no place in Sandino's revolutionary lineage. My feeling for the revolution came instead through the Marxist ideas that inspired the Frente's leaders. And it was in the realm of ideas that Sandino was weakest.

While Sandino was surely one of the world's great anti-imperialists, he was neither a Marxist nor a socialist. In fact, he was a political oddball. Before going to Nicaragua, I read something about Sandino that the Frente left out of its official story—the part about Sandino being a mystic, a visionary, a hearer of voices, a believer in reincarnation. Sandino was Nicaragua's official representative of the Magnetic-Spiritualist School of the Universal Commune, which blended the mysticism of Zoroastrianism, Kabbalah, and Spiritism with the politics of anarchism and communism. The result was a "spiritism of Light and Truth," a new philosophy that was supposed to supersede all existing religions by ushering in the final stage of human history. Halfway through his fight against the Americans, Sandino replaced his rebel army's seal—a machete-wielding peasant beheading a U.S. Marine—with the symbol of the Universal Commune: a pyramid, a star of David, and an anchor surrounded by a sunburst. He even issued his own "Manifesto of Light and Truth" in a letter to his followers (translated by Robert Edgar in *Sandino: The Testimony of a Nicaraguan Patriot, 1921–1934*): "The honor has fallen to us that in Nicaragua we have been chosen by Divine Justice to begin the prosecution of injustice on earth. Do not fear, my brothers and sisters, and be certain, very certain, and perfectly certain that very soon we will have our final triumph in Nicaragua, with which the wick of the 'Proletarian Explosion' against the imperialists of the earth will be lit."

Unlike the image of Che, however, or the red and black colors of the Frente Sandinista, the symbol of Sandino never lit my political wick—until I found myself standing in the plaza and staring at his gigantic portrait while listening to our speaker issue a final warning to the American imperialists. At that moment I felt the serene but steely defiance in Sandino's face, a defiance that was based on the simple but irrefutable demand that my country leave his country alone. For the first time, I truly saw the United States through the eyes of those who were vulnerable to its devastating power.

A shiver ran down my spine. The speaker had just raised his fist and shouted Sandino's famous cry "¡Patria libre!" (A free country!), to which the crowd thundered "¡O morir!" (Or death!).

6

We filed out of the plaza in a line several blocks long and a dozen people wide. A couple of marchers banged drums. Some waved the red and black Sandinista flag. Others carried placards, one of which read: "¡Como en Vietnam les romperemos la argolla!" (We'll bust their balls—just like in Vietnam!).

Everyone was screaming slogans. Chants of "¡No pasarán!" (They won't get through!) warned the world that no one—not the contras, not the Americans, not anybody—would penetrate the defenses of the revolution. Shouts of "¡Viva Sandino!" "¡Viva el Che!" "¡Viva la Revolución Sandinista!" elicited collective replies of "¡Viva!" Cries of "¡Patria libre!" called forth "¡O morir!" A lone, piercing scream of "¡Gringos asesinos!" (Murderous gringos!) was answered by a hundred unified voices screaming "¡Fuera de Grenada!" (Get out of Grenada!). The names of Sandinista martyrs—like Silvio Mayorga, Germán Pomares, and Francisco Buitrago—were called out and honored with the reply "¡Presente!"

I was the only one not shouting. Everyone else had shouted the slogans of their revolution a thousand times before. They all had siblings, cousins, or friends who died fighting the dictator. And they all knew someone who was now fighting the contras. So even after five months in Nicaragua and in the middle of a march against American imperialism, I could not bring myself to shout what I knew were *their* slogans. But I almost did. For at that very moment I truly hated my government and was ready to stand up for Nicaragua's right to its revolution.

We left the obliterated downtown and began walking past single buildings, then past clusters of buildings, and eventually past whole blocks of one- and two-story buildings coated in whitewash. We finally merged with thousands of other marchers in a spacious intersection. Before long I got separated from my colleagues and left the thickening crowd to watch it from the front steps of a nearby house.

Right in front of me was a large group of young men and women from the Sandinista Youth Organization, whose stated goal was to prepare "a new man for a new society." Most of its forty or fifty thousand members came from better than average families in the bigger cities. But anyone could join. All you needed was a revolutionary outlook and a willingness to sign up for a work brigade or train with a militia. You could become a *militante* after six months of demonstrated commitment.

The two or three hundred youth in front of me had surely graduated to militant status. Most were dressed in olive green pants and white T-shirts. Some wore military caps. A few carried their AK-47s. All were shouting "¡Un solo ejército! ¡Un solo ejército!"—There is only one army, a revolutionary army, the Sandinista army. They were right. The nation's armed forces were called the Sandinista army rather than the Nicaraguan army. Similarly, the nation's police were called the Sandinista police rather than city, county, or federal police. No one there that day saw any danger in a partisan army. We saw only a people's army defending the people's revolution.

All at once the young Sandinistas began jumping up and down to a new chant: "¡Somos Sandinistas, pa'lante, pa'lante, y al que no le guste que aguante, que aguante!" The chant had a powerful rhythm punctuated by the rhyming words *pa'lante* and *aguante*. It had an equally powerful message: We are Sandinistas, we are taking charge, and it is just too bad if you don't like it. A minute later they were screaming another slogan: "¡Seremos como el Che! ¡Seremos como el Che! (We'll be like Che! We'll be like Che!)." They must have chanted it fifteen or twenty times.

Young people composed the Frente's single biggest group of supporters. They were also the most enthusiastic. Not for nothing did the director of the Center include them in his "third social force of national liberation." He even called them a revolutionary force in their own right. "Just as *Sandinista ideology and Nicaraguan youth* was the formula for defeating a dictatorship," he wrote, "so is it now the formula for guiding our society toward a superior form of life." If you had to reduce the revolution to a single formula, "Sandinista ideology and Nicaraguan youth" was as good as any. It meant turning teenagers into socialists by teaching them the basics of Marxism. Like Che said (in *Notes on Man and Socialism in Cuba*, which everyone at the Center had read), "Youth is the malleable clay from which the new man can be shaped without any of the old faults."

In my own small way, I was putting the director's formula and Che's dictum into action. For three or four months I had been helping three Sandinista youths read a long and difficult book called *Revolutionary Theory and Practice in Nicaragua: A Primer on Marxism*. The leader of their Youth Brigade had told them to read it.

The primer is described as "a basic course in revolutionary theory" designed to help "the exploited people of Nicaragua realize their dreams and carry out their struggles." To that end, the book explains the basic ideas of Marxism. And with the didacticism of a true primer, each of its chapters poses final review questions:

Why is Marxism also called scientific socialism? What do you think about that?

What is the logic of the capitalist system?

Why is the worker alienated from the capitalist process of production? Do you know anyone who is alienated?

Why does Marx say that class is the "motor" of history? Can you see any concrete examples of the motor of history working in your community?

Explain the following phrase: "Sandino's anti-imperialist struggle shows that there is no contradiction between Marxist internationalism and Sandinista nationalism."

What are the two fundamental ideas of Marx's materialist theory of history? Do you agree?

What are the differences between Hegel's dialectical method and Marx's dialectical method? How well do you think Marx's dialectical method works?

We discussed those very questions—for which I, of course, had the answers. With absolute sincerity, I tried to help my younger comrades understand how the class struggle drives history and why socialism is a scientific idea rather than a utopian ideal. I even tried explaining the differences between the dialectical methods of Marx and Hegel, though I was merely showing off because I knew that my pupils were not ready for the dialectic.

Most of the time, though, I was too infatuated with the image of myself teaching Marxism to Sandinistas to notice that they were learning merely to mouth the phrases of what constituted a revolutionary consciousness. All they were learning, in other words, was to believe that the Frente was the *vanguardia* of the revolution, that Nicaragua's *burguesía* was the enemy of the people, and that *capitalismo* was bad, *imperialismo* worse, and *socialismo* the ultimate form of liberation.

The few times that I allowed myself to notice how little of the primer my pupils actually understood, I took refuge in the words of a comandante. "While it is pretty easy," he wrote in an essay called "The Ideological Struggle," "for us revolutionaries to take over economic power—that is, to take over the material base and true power of the society—it is harder, and it takes more time, to take over the ideological power of society: that intangible power over the mentality of men." On at least one occasion I didn't even need the excuse of "more time"—the excuse we used for everything that was not quite right with the revolution. I was so sure of the truth in Marx's ideas that I told myself it was all right for my young friends to act on them before they even grasped them.

So instead of seeing two or three hundred rabid twenty-year-olds jabbing their fists in the air to punctuate the words of slogans they didn't understand, I saw Sandinista youth ready to defend a revolution that was rightfully theirs.

That night it was my turn to do revolutionary vigilance, an all-night block watch organized by the neighborhood's Sandinista Defense Committee. Nearly every village and neighborhood in Nicaragua had a Defense Committee. Some committees had a lot of support, others hardly any. Most were like the one in my neighborhood, which had the support of 5 or 10 percent of the people, about two or three households per block. Defense Committees handled emergencies, distributed ration cards for rice, beans, and cooking oil, and verified the revolutionary credentials of people seeking government jobs or permits. Mainly, though, they were exactly what the Frente called them: "the eyes and ears of the revolution."

I did revolutionary vigilance every couple of weeks with my next-door neighbor, Elena, a plump, good-looking, twenty-seven-year-old single mother of three. She made half of her living by selling beer and soft drinks that she bought wholesale, chilled in her refrigerator, and sold to the many neighbors on our block who did not have refrigerators. She earned the rest of her money by finishing the raw handles and broom heads that she bought from a carpenter down the street. With the help of her eight-year-old son, she sanded and painted them before gluing tufts of bristles into the many small holes that had been drilled into the broom heads. She sold the finished brooms to an old man in a run-down station wagon.

Like Elena, most of my neighbors had six years of schooling and made modest livings—as seamstresses, car mechanics, food makers, hairdressers, taxi drivers, small-time merchants, and backyard carpenters and metalworkers. And like Elena, they lived in small houses made of cement floors, sheet-metal roofs, and stucco walls that were coated in whitewash or painted with pale blues and greens. But Elena was one of only two people on our block who did revolutionary vigilance.

When Osvaldo first visited my place and saw that it was furnished with two rocking chairs, a transistor radio, a mattress, and an end table—but no stove, telephone, refrigerator, television, or dinner table—he said, "You're not only living with the proletariat, you're living like a proletarian!" Osvaldo didn't know that I was merely living like a graduate student, but he was right to say that I was living with Nicaragua's version of an urban proletariat.

Like proletarians everywhere, however, my neighbors were far less likely than better-off and well-educated people to be revolutionaries. And most of the proletarians who believed enough in the Frente to do vigilance did not see the revolution as people like Osvaldo saw it.

Elena, for example, could name only two of the nine comandantes. She knew nothing of the various ministries. She sometimes listened to the Frente's radio station but never read its newspaper. She had heard of Sandino but knew only that he had driven away the Yankees in the time of her grandparents. And she never talked about socialism, a new society, or the agrarian reform.

Yet she liked the *muchachos*, as she called the Sandinistas. She liked them, she said, because they had thrown out the dictator and stood up for ordinary people against the *ricos*, whom she sometimes called the *burguesía*. Elena never talked of throwing out the rich altogether, but she did like the idea of confiscating the property of the bourgeoisie and giving it to poor people. As a longtime renter, she supported a Sandinista proposal to let renters apply all of their past rent to the purchase price of the house, which the landlord would be required to sell should the tenant want to buy it. As a mother, she liked the subsidized price of beans, rice, and cooking oil, and she appreciated the new primary school in the neighborhood. As a resident of the barrio, she was happy to see the Frente paving a section of dirt streets full of mosquito-breeding puddles and lined by wooden shanties. Her only complaint was about the endless bickering between the comandantes and the country's archbishop. "The Sandinistas are not on God's side," she once told me, "so I have to hope that he's on theirs."

One of the comandantes told the Sandinista newspaper *Barricada* (Barricade) that "the worker is in the dark in terms of knowledge, but he has a class-based intuition about who his enemies are." The comment made sense to me. Elena had only a vague understanding of the revolution, but she resented rich people. And she had taken what I condescendingly admired as the big step of turning her "class-based intuition" into support for the Frente. So I felt privileged to be doing vigilance with the real thing: a working-class supporter of the revolution.

The contras were a hundred miles away and Managua was perfectly safe, but the Frente still wanted its Defense Committees to do vigilance. A part of me suspected that doing vigilance, in Managua anyway, was more about showing one's loyalty to the revolution than watching for its enemies. The lack of real danger made me want to believe the rumor that a couple of contras had been caught a year earlier trying to blow up a nearby bridge. It also made me exaggerate the importance of an ongoing war of graffiti in the neighborhood.

A few months before, somebody painted the name Edén on a stop sign. Edén Pastora was a popular Sandinista leader who defected to the contras. Someone then painted *traidor* (traitor) over *Edén*. More ominously, the warnings "Reactionaries beware" and "A contra lives here" were scrawled across several houses the day after the word *comunista* had been written on the door of a committee leader. Several nights later, someone painted over the warnings. And so it went. The idea of catching a counterrevolutionary in the act

Michael Johns

of writing reactionary graffiti added a hint of danger to our tranquil nights of watching for enemies of the revolution.

But we had no need to manufacture our fear on the night of the invasion of Grenada. As I left my house at eleven to sit out with Elena, I remembered one of my ministry colleagues warning us to stay alert. "You never know with the Americans," he said. "They can do whatever they want and when you least expect it. They might invade us tonight because they think that we think that they are tied up in Grenada."

Elena was already outside. She was sitting in a chair on the cement slab that formed the floor of her house and extended three feet beyond its front wall to the edge of the narrow street. I sat down on the slab with my back to her house. I had not seen Elena that day. With a mischievous smile she said, "If your gringos invade Nicaragua, you better hope they don't mistake you for a Sandinista!"

For the next hour or so Elena and I watched nervously as one neighbor after another closed the door and shut off the lights. Before long the entire street was dark. And it was very quiet. We had done vigilance five or six times before, but we had never been scared.

Ricardo's arrival made it scarier. He was a short but well-built twenty-year-old soldier in a counterinsurgency unit called an Irregular Warfare Battalion. It used helicopters to drop small squads into rugged terrain where they would hunt down contras. Ricardo fought for two weeks at a time before coming home for a month of rest. He usually came back with fungal rot on his hands or feet. Sometimes he returned with one fewer soldier in his squad.

Ricardo was proud to be in the Sandinista army. He liked the comandantes and hated the contras. He sometimes mouthed revolutionary jargon. But he was more soldier than Sandinista, a simple barrio kid who needed a job.

I once made the mistake of giving him the memoir of a big-time Sandinista, Omar Cabezas, who had trained guerrilla fighters in the mountains during the war against Somoza's dictatorship. It was a mistake because Ricardo couldn't relate to the ideas and ideals of the Frente's college-educated revolutionaries.

When Ricardo showed no interest in the author's discussion of revolutionary politics, I tried to get his reaction to a passage that was all at once visceral, political, and philosophical. So I read aloud from *Fire from the Mountain: The Making of a Sandinista*:

> As if the mountain and the mud, the mud, and also the rain and the loneliness, as if all these things were cleansing us of a bunch of bourgeois defects, a whole series of vices; we learned to be humble, because you alone are not worth shit up there. You learn to be simple; you learn to value principles. You learn to appreciate the strictly human values that of necessity emerge in that environment. And little by little all our faults faded out. That was why we said that the genesis of the new man was in the FSLN. The new man began to be born with fungus infections and with his feet oozing worms; the new man began to be born with loneliness and eaten alive by mosquitoes; he began to be born stinking. That's the outer part, because inside, by dint of violent shocks day after day, the new man was being born with the freshness of the mountains. A man—it might seem incredible—but an open, unegotistical man, no longer petty—a tender man who sacrifices for others, who suffers when others suffer and who also laughs when others laugh.

I looked up to see Ricardo smiling. "I know all about the mud and the rain and the mosquitoes," he said, "and I always stink and get rashes and infections when I'm up there. But I've never felt like a new man." He laughed sheepishly and said, "That's for the big Sandinistas."

From then on we stuck to talking about girls and baseball, to listening to Michael Jackson's *Thriller* on Ricardo's boom box, and to playing basketball on a makeshift backboard and rim attached to a nearby telephone pole. The differences between us put limits on our friendship, but I always worried about Ricardo when he was fighting and felt relieved when he came home.

When Ricardo was not in the mountains, he always stopped by to chat while Elena and I did vigilance. Once he sat out all night with us. But not until the invasion of Grenada did he bring his AK-47.

And no sooner had he sat down next to me and put his rifle between us than he said, "Brother," in English, as many Nicaraguans did, though pronouncing it BRO-there, "I don't want to see Marines here. They're not mercenaries like the contras. They're the best fighters in the world. And besides, they're Americans. I don't want to fight Americans. No," he said, shaking his head, "we Nicaraguans don't want to fight Americans."

Nor did I. But I was too caught up in the day's momentum and too invested in being an American revolutionary to wonder whether I really ought to be watching for U.S. Marines—never mind what I would do if I saw them.

I hardly noticed any more the tens of thousands of revolutionary symbols that covered the capital city and made sure you knew who was running the place and what they wanted to do with it. Over the months, the symbols had faded from my view to become the equivalent of pleasant wall hangings or favorite background music. Yet I couldn't stop looking at them on the way to breakfast after our night of vigilance.

Silhouettes of Sandino and slogans like "¡No pasarán!" marked the doors and walls of a quarter of the houses on my block. A row of big, free-standing, block-lettered signs dominated a stretch of the adjacent commercial street. They said "All Arms to the People for the Defense of the Revolution," "Long Live the Proletariat," and "The FSLN is the Vanguard." An entire side of a small furniture factory was covered with the statement "Every Factory Is a Fortress for the Construction of Socialism." A mural on a local office of the Sandinista Workers Federation depicted Sandino holding a machete in one hand and the Frente's banner in the other. Dead American soldiers lay at his feet. The accompanying slogan read, "Sandino Lives, the Struggle Continues." The first of two billboards showed the faces of four Sandinistas who had been killed in the early days of the fight against Somoza; a main point in the Frente's political platform was "to cultivate gratitude and eternal veneration for the revolution's martyrs." The second billboard showed the face of Karl Marx. A half year earlier the Frente held a conference to honor the hundredth anniversary of his death.

Not since my first weeks in Nicaragua had I looked so closely at the revolution's signage. What had charmed and excited me in those first few weeks, however, and then faded so nicely into a kind of reassuring political wallpaper, suddenly seemed strange and uncertain. Some part of my brain was seeing the revolution's signs and symbols for the slogans and propaganda that they really were. And I wasn't sure what to make of it.

A few minutes later I was sitting in a small restaurant and feeling similarly estranged from the Sandinista newspaper *Barricada*. The Frente produced large runs of its newspaper on a new East German press and sold each paper for about a penny. What it couldn't sell, it gave away. You could always find a small stack of the day's paper in every bar, store, school, bus station, government office, and movie theater. And in a country short of basic goods, *Barricada* became everyone's emergency (and many people's daily) toilet paper, which gave opponents of the Frente an easy quip about the value of its newspaper.

From my first day in Nicaragua I was thrilled to be in a country whose biggest newspaper was a revolutionary newspaper. I liked the paper's nervy masthead, which displayed the words "Official Organ of the FSLN" just below the title and between a big-hatted Sandino and a beret-wearing Sandinista who was firing a rifle from behind a barricade. I liked the editors' description of their work: "journalism by the Vanguard for a revolutionary people." And I liked their idea of its being "an ideological weapon for the masses." Although it was clear to me that *Barricada* was less professional and more political than the *New York Times*, I found it to be no less truthful. In fact, I thought *Barricada* was more honest than the *Times* because it was so explicit about its politics— a revolutionary politics that I, of course, saw as a truth in itself.

Arming the people with ideas meant delivering each and every day a concentrated and vitalizing dose of revolution. To that end, a typical day's headlines maligned the contras—

"Sandinista Army Slaughters Ten Counterrevolutionary Dogs in the North"; trumpeted the revolution's progress—"Just Another Weekend for the Agrarian Reform—100,000 Acres to the Peasants!"; proclaimed worldwide support for the Sandinistas—"Economic Accord Shows France's Solidarity with the Revolution"; warned of a possible U.S. invasion—"This Gentle Land Will Become a Hell-fire for Yankee Invaders"; and highlighted the revolutionary spirit of Nicaraguans— "Six Thousand Students Volunteer for the Coffee Harvest."

The morning after the invasion of Grenada, however, *Barricada* had just one headline—"Our Rifles Are Ready to Mow Down the Invaders." The accompanying photos showed Sandinista crowds marching in protest. One of the captions read, "The people of Sandino with clenched fists and cries of '¡No pasarán!' marched in solidarity with Grenada against the Yankee invader." Another said, "With burning hearts, cool heads, and rifles ready for the Yankee invaders, the masses took to the streets in a combative mood."

While imagining myself as a dot in one of the overhead shots of the crowds, I looked again at the giant headline and glanced back and forth between the photos and their captions, and then, for just a moment, I felt far away from it all—as though it were happening to somebody else in some other place.

9

Later that morning I was taking a break from digging the now-waist-deep trench when Sergio came into the office to get something. He said I looked tired. His comment gave me the chance to tell him that I had spent the night doing vigilance. As an American who came late to the revolution, I always felt the need to prove myself. So I let colleagues know, as casually as I could, whenever I did vigilance or led a discussion of the *Primer on Marxism* or spent a weekend painting the cinder-block walls of the elementary school in my neighborhood. And now, with the fear of invasion running high, I felt an even greater need to show Sergio that I was no fair-weather sympathizer.

"It's good that you did vigilance," he said, "and that you aren't making plans to leave—like some *internacionalistas*." He then looked me straight in the eye and said, "But if you are a true internationalist, then you should give up your American citizenship, become Nicaraguan, and join the Frente." He held his stare for a few seconds before leaving.

I couldn't tell whether he was sincere or toying with me or calling my bluff, but his comment bothered me the rest of the day. I never seriously considered giving up my American citizenship, but I did fall prey to the notion that if I were truly a Marxist I ought to commit myself wholly to the revolution. And I kept thinking of two South Americans who had actually renounced their citizenship to become Sandinistas. I even tried to picture myself living in Nicaragua forever. That I could not see myself as a Nicaraguan should have expunged the idea of becoming one, but I needed an excuse to finally get rid of it. "What if I become Nicaraguan," I asked myself, "and the country someday falls back into the hands of non-revolutionaries? Where would I be then?"

I was fully aware that my commitment to the revolution was unproven and open to question, but what made me particularly vulnerable to Sergio's challenge was that it came from him rather than some strident or doctrinaire Sandinista. In fact, Sergio was the only Sandinista I knew who poked fun at the Frente.

Every few weeks the Frente's big theorists identified a new *coyuntura*, or critical conjuncture. They detected such conjunctures in the class struggle, in the war of imperialist aggression, in the revolutionary consciousness of the people, and in the dialectical relationship between the vanguard and the masses. One theorist had even detected a critical conjuncture in the final crisis of global capitalism. The search for conjunctures is natural in a transition to socialism, when every incident or moment assumes a fateful importance for those trying to control the revolution's destiny.

Several of us were eating lunch one day when somebody mentioned the latest conjuncture: the agrarian reform's role in changing the political awareness of the peasants. "Yet another coyuntura," sighed Sergio. "Before you know it, one of the Frente's *profundistas* [deep thinkers] is going to depict a comandante's brushing his teeth or screwing his wife as a new coyuntura." I laughed and Sergio beamed, but none of our lunch companions thought it was funny.

It takes almost total certainty to believe in a revolutionary transition to socialism. And too much certainty squashes the skepticism required for a roomy sense of humor. But Sergio was funny and irreverent, which made me take his challenge to become a Nicaraguan more seriously than I should have.

10

I almost asked the bus driver to let me off as we approached the Center on our way out of Managua. Earlier that morning, I had heard one of the comandantes telling Radio Sandino that the Frente was "going to defend every inch of Nicaragua by turning the country into one big trench to trap the Yankee invaders." That kind of talk made it hard to go about my daily business. But if one part of me wanted the security of being with my colleagues, the other part of me wanted to avoid another day of digging in the trench and fretting about an invasion and remembering what Sergio had said. So I stayed on the bus with the hope of doing a regular day of social science for the revolution—and avoiding the uncomfortable question of whether I would actually fight for it.

A minute later we were in open countryside. The long rainy season had turned tens of thousands of tiny pastures and cornfields into a flowing carpet of green that was interrupted only by the distant shapes of huts and hamlets and the crisscrossing lines of cart roads and tree-lined streams. And the only interruption to my enjoyment of the gently sloping scenery was the inevitable head-jerking stench of a dog in the ripest state of decay. I never saw fewer than three or four rotting dogs along this twenty-mile stretch of intercity highway, which in reality was a country road with no shoulders, no center stripe, and no shortage of drivers willing to pass with the tiniest of openings.

Watching the landscape from a bus was one of my favorite

things to do in Nicaragua. I especially liked watching it from the bottom step of the front door, which was always open. Some buses didn't even have doors. And the bottom step was almost always available because hardly anyone wanted to stand there. A teenager standing next to me once lost his grip on a slow left turn. He fell off and struggled mightily to keep his balance for five or six desperate strides before finally hitting the ground and rolling over a few times.

I first stood on the bottom step of a bus simply to avoid the sweaty heat and jam-packed aisles, but I was immediately hooked on the clear view, the fresh air, and the thrill of tempting the lax rules, the shoddy infrastructure, and the fatalistic spontaneity of the Nicaraguan culture that the Frente was trying to turn into socialism.

I got off in the city of Masaya and walked five miles to the town of Catarina. I walked fast and resolutely, as if to keep ahead of the fear of invasion that was dogging me from the back of my mind. The narrow dirt road cut through horse pastures, stands of avocado trees, fields of just-picked corn, and three or four villages made up of a dozen one-room, dirt-floor, tin-roof houses surrounded by sweet-smelling citrus trees.

Catarina was a dozen square blocks of whitewashed buildings whose doors and shutters were painted in pastel blues, browns, and yellows. There were more horses than cars in the town's streets, half of which had been newly paved in flagstone. Some of the townspeople worked as farm hands, but most of them grew flowers or made baskets and pots for the traders who sold them in Masaya and Managua.

The door was open to the office of the Asociación de Trabajadores del Campo (Rural Workers Union). It looked like the ten or fifteen other offices I had visited. Two desks were pushed against the far wall, and a long, ratty couch and three old chairs filled out the place. Piles of papers and pamphlets occupied the corner behind the door. Revolutionary posters covered the peeling walls. Two naked lightbulbs hung from the ceiling. Nobody was there, so I shut the door and sat outside against the building, trying not to think about the United States invading Nicaragua.

A half hour later a brown-skinned man in his late twenties came toward the office. His mustache and chin patch were so thin that he might never have shaved. He was wearing army boots, light-blue polyester pants, and a white, untucked, short-sleeve shirt. His baseball cap said Industriales, the name of a famous Cuban baseball team. Nicaraguans loved baseball, and there were a lot of Cubans in Nicaragua.

He was one of the Rural Workers Union's three hundred cadres. They all came from poor peasant families and rarely had more than six years of schooling. Many of them had fought with the Frente against Somoza. Now they were organizing the union's fifty thousand members, all of whom were campesinos with too little land—if they had any land at all—to make a living from farming. So they worked as seasonal laborers on coffee, cotton, tobacco, sugarcane, and vegetable farms.

I introduced myself as an American doing a study of the cotton and coffee harvests for the Agrarian Reform Ministry. "Welcome, *compañero*," he said. He shook my hand and invited me inside. We sat in the chairs at the desks.

Before telling him about my study, I asked about his work. He launched immediately into a concise analysis of his Rural Workers Union and the Frente's agrarian reform, which were, in effect, the same thing. In a soft but confident voice he began by telling me that the union was doing its best to raise the revolutionary consciousness of the campesinos. A quarter of the region's landless peasants had joined the union, he told me, and most of its members had joined their village Defense Committees. The more the campesinos learn to see their class position as rural workers, he said, the more they realize that the only way to advance their interests is by struggling against the bourgeoisie.

But it was hard, he went on, to change the "petty bourgeois ways of campesinos. Most of them would rather work a small plot of their own or rent a piece of land than join a co-operative or a collective farm. And a lot of them still trust the Catholic Church and its reactionary archbishop more than they trust the Frente and its comandantes. Some campesinos can't even stop themselves from kowtowing to the very landowners who have been exploiting them for years."

His tone was objective rather than judgmental, and he played down the slow pace of ideological change among the peasants. "It's politically impossible," he told me, "to expropriate the bourgeoisie all at once. Besides, we still haven't developed the necessary technical and management skills to efficiently run our existing co-operatives and collective farms. So we have plenty of time to do our political work among the peasants. That's why it's best, at least for now, to let the progressive elements of the bourgeoisie continue to run their farms."

After hearing him speak, I wasn't surprised to see a small book among the reports and pamphlets on his desk. It was *A Little Glossary of the Agrarian Reform*. I had seen *A Little Glossary* at the Center and in three or four of the union's offices. The Agrarian Reform Ministry had written it specifically for the Rural Workers Union. Like the Frente itself, the ministry was made up almost entirely of educated men (and some women) from the cities. So it needed to train rural cadres who could win over the peasants and carry out agrarian reform; *A Little Glossary* defined the reform as "a revolutionary program designed to overhaul the work process and property relations of the countryside."

The glossary is an ABC of Marxism. Entries include bourgeoisie, class struggle, exploitation, imperialism, mode of production, national liberation, petty bourgeoisie, profit, proletariat, rent, surplus value, and vanguard. Capitalism is defined as "a mode of production based on the exploitation of workers by capitalists" and communism as "a mode of production without social classes or the exploitation of man by man."

Most of the entries are illustrated with pencil sketches.

The bourgeoisie is drawn as a mean-looking man watching his toiling workers through dark glasses. The concept of rent is brought to life by an oppressed peasant giving money to a fat man wearing a sports jacket and holding a fistful of cash. A Sandinista co-operative is depicted as an orderly village full of proud peasants working together in harmony.

The glossary is small, crude, and illustrated, but it provided rural cadres with a clear and powerful picture of the world—the very same picture, for all intents and purposes, that Sergio, Osvaldo, and I had formed in our own minds with the help of hundreds of books.

But it was clear to me that this particular cadre had read a lot more than the glossary, for he was far more articulate and sure of himself than the other cadres I had met. They all spoke the vocabulary of revolution, but none of them spoke it with the mastery of the man sitting next to me.

He wrapped up his ten-minute talk with a perfect summary of the Rural Workers Union—the kind of summary I expected to hear only from people like Sergio and Osvaldo. "The first phase began the moment the revolution took power," he said, "and is still our main focus: getting better wages and working conditions for poor campesinos. The second began a little later but is well under way. We are trying to place the most politically advanced peasants on co-operatives and collectives formed out of properties confiscated from the reactionary sectors of the bourgeoisie. The third phase is still a ways off. The union's job will be to support the Frente's expropriation of the bourgeoisie in general, and to help the campesinos turn it into the property of the people."

At the end of his speech I remembered Osvaldo calling union cadres "the organic intellectuals of the agrarian reform." The phrase "organic intellectual" comes from an Italian Marxist named Antonio Gramsci, whose *Prison Notebooks* constituted required reading for the Sandinista intelligentsia. The organic intellectual is that special worker who instinctively grasps the Marxian categories—even if he learned them from glossaries and primers—and who, more

importantly, uses those categories to fight for the true interests of his class rather than letting upper-class Marxists do it
for him.

As I began telling the cadre about my research, I pictured
him as an organic intellectual working tirelessly for the revolution while I spent my days taking pleasant walks on back
roads looking for people who, like this very cadre, could help
me with my study. I then worried that my study wouldn't
teach him a thing about the harvests, which he knew inti-
mately but I would only ever know from the distance of social science. Even more unsettling was seeing myself as a
mere outsider on the edge of the revolution.

So I was relieved, even grateful, when the cadre said that
it would be very useful to know how many people picked
coffee and cotton, where they came from, and what other
kinds of work they did. He then told me exactly what I had
always had to spell out for other cadres. "It would be useful,"
he said, "because we have a problem internal to the agrarian
reform—the more peasants we put on co-operatives and collective farms, the fewer people we have to harvest the coffee,
cotton, and sugarcane that bring in our foreign exchange. So
we have to be careful how we go about giving away land and
organizing labor."

I unfolded a map of the region and asked him to point out
nearby villages where harvest workers lived. Before looking
at the map he pulled two unfiltered cigarettes from the pack
in his shirt pocket. I didn't smoke, but situations like this
seemed to call for it. So I inhaled just enough to blow a rela-
tively smooth stream of smoke through my nose. We leaned
over the desk and looked at the map while smoking our cigarettes. He had a rough idea of how many people from several
villages had gone to the harvests in previous years. And he
agreed to give me a hand with my study.

After ten weeks of talking to union cadres, Sandinista politicos, and labor contractors throughout the region, I had
a pretty good idea of where the coffee and cotton pickers
came from. Now I was ready to do an actual count during

the upcoming harvests that would begin in a few weeks. My plan was to visit all of the towns and villages where harvest workers were known to live and to get the exact numbers of this year's harvesters from the leaders of Sandinista Defense Committees, who knew everyone in their communities.

There were some fourteen thousand harvest workers, however, and they lived in two hundred hamlets and villages spread over five hundred square miles. So I asked the cadre for the favor I had asked of several others: to count the harvesters in two or three out-of-the-way places in his district. I gave him a form on which to record the number of harvesters, what crops they picked, and whether they were men, women, or children. He agreed to have it ready for me in two months.

After we shook hands, I asked him if he knew any cadres in the small town up the road. "Yes," he said, "but they're busy helping their Sandinista Defense Committee get ready for an invasion." He said it as though it were just another day in the life of a revolutionary labor organizer.

But then he added, "I'll tell you something, though. I hope every American I meet is carrying a little green backpack like yours"—backpacks were still foreign objects to most Nicaraguans—"instead of an M-16." He then paused for a few seconds before saying, with a wry but sympathetic smile, "I'm sure you do too."

I answered with a smile of my own, as though I wanted to convince the both of us that even though I was scared, I was fully prepared to defend Nicaragua's revolution against Yankee invaders.

11

Six or seven hours later I was reading an essay in *The Complete Works of Che Guevara* when a member of the neighborhood's Sandinista Defense Committee knocked on my door. He had a wispy mustache and the small potbelly that was typical of Nicaraguan men in their mid-thirties.

"The Frente is setting up a militia in our section of the neighborhood," he said. "Training begins tomorrow afternoon at four. We'll meet in the schoolyard. Will you be there?"

I hesitated for a second before saying, as though I had no choice in the matter and despite feeling like I might be getting in over my head, "Yes. Of course. I'll be there."

He nodded with approval before adding my name to a list in his spiral notebook. He then asked for my address. Because Managua's streets had no names and its houses had no numbers—which might explain why there were no maps of the city—addresses were built around landmarks: "Barrio Altagracia; from the lumberyard, three blocks toward the lake, twenty-five yards in and on the right." I signed next to my name. We shook hands and said good night.

Just like that I had joined a militia. I didn't know why. And I was afraid to think about it. So I went back to reading Che.

12

"On behalf of the Frente Sandinista, I applaud your eagerness to defend the revolution in this new coyuntura of the imperialist war against Third World struggles for national liberation." That was how a young, cocky, third-tier Sandinista wearing fatigues and a side arm began his short speech on our first day of training in the neighborhood schoolyard.

I smiled when he said "coyuntura" because it reminded me of Sergio's quip about Sandinista intellectuals depicting everything from brushing their teeth to screwing their wives as critical conjunctures. Yet I could not help thinking that the thirty people standing beside me had no idea what it meant. Few of them had finished high school. None of them had joined the Frente or worked for one of its ministries. And if some of my fellow militiamen did revolutionary vigilance, it did not look like any of them belonged to the Sandinista Youth Brigade, to the Sandinista Workers Federation, or to another Sandinista group that might have taught them the meaning of a word like "coyuntura."

Our speaker was barely into his talk when he spotted me in the crowd and asked me who I was. "I'm working for the Ministry of Agrarian Reform," I said.

"Well," he announced, "here we have an American compañero who came to Nicaragua simply to help the agrarian reform but is now willing to fight for the revolution against the imperialism of his own country." He called me an *internacionalista de verdad*, a true internationalist. I was living proof, he told us, that Americans can overcome the imperialist ideology of their country to join the cause of national liberation.

I had always enjoyed being seen as a revolutionary American in Sandinista Nicaragua, so I was particularly pleased to be singled out for high praise at this poignant moment. And I made sure to appear solemn and act as though I was merely doing my revolutionary duty. Yet something about the speaker bothered me. He had every right to announce that I was ready to defend the revolution against my own country—I had joined a militia, after all—but it seemed presumptuous somehow.

He went on to say that today's Nicaraguans were like yesterday's Americans "who had fought so valiantly to free themselves from the oppressive yoke of British colonialism. Only now, it is the Americans who are the oppressors. But no," he said, correcting himself while looking at me, "it is not the American people who are the oppressors, it's the American government. For the American people understand that Nicaragua is trying to create a free society; the American people understand that their own government fears Nicaragua's revolution only because the Frente Sandinista is setting an anti-imperialist example for the rest of the world; the American people understand that their government is breaking international law by supporting the counterrevolution. And what's more," he said, barely containing his delight with the phrases rolling so easily off his tongue, "the American people are starting to understand that they themselves need to carry out a revolution against their own tyrannical government, which is oppressing its own people as well as those of the Third World. Didn't Thomas Jefferson himself, the writer of the American constitution, say that 'the tree of liberty must be refreshed from time to time with the blood of patriots and tyrants'?"

Sandinista intellectuals liked throwing America's revolutionary history in its face. They also liked separating the American government, which was bad, from its people, who were good or, at worst, naive. Most of all, they liked harping on America's problems—the racism, the decadence, the homelessness, the drugs, the political apathy, the lasting shame of the colossal debacle of Vietnam—while exalting the Frente for building a morally superior society in poor little Nicaragua.

And I liked watching them do it. For I hated my government and felt at fault for its actions. Listening to Sandinistas criticize my country had the atoning quality of doing penance.

But this particular Sandinista was getting on my nerves. He was slick and ambitious and too conscious of himself as a leader. At one point I even suspected him of mouthing phrases he had heard from smarter Sandinistas. And when he used the word "coyuntura" for a second time, I was sure he enjoyed knowing that few of us knew what it meant.

I knew some disagreeable Sandinistas. I knew some stupid ones, too. But they never got on my nerves. In fact, almost nothing got on my nerves until the invasion of Grenada. For nearly five months my experience of the revolution had been like that of a lucky tourist: passing through the finest scenery, stopping in the best spots for just the right length of time, and seeing only the attractive surface of things—and all thanks to the Marxist guidebook in my head.

The invasion of Grenada changed everything. On consecutive days I had dug a trench, been tested by Sergio, and joined a militia. I experienced more of the revolution in those three days than I had in the previous five months. All at once I was pulled beneath the surface of the revolution and drawn right down into it. And if standing among my militia comrades made me want to believe even more in the revolution that I was readying myself to defend, the need to shield myself from the possibility of real danger had the opposite effect of making me pay more attention to it.

Our speaker finished his talk by introducing the three men who had been standing behind him. They would lead our training, he told us, which would begin the next afternoon and consist of two hours per day for three weeks. He then exhorted us to fight for Nicaragua as heroically as the

Cuban internationalists who were working in Grenada had
fought the invading imperialists. He ended our meeting by
leading collective shouts of "¡No pasarán!" and "¡Patria libre
o morir!"

I had never before shouted a slogan in Nicaragua. That
was for Sandinistas, I told myself. But I was now in too deep
not to shout.

13

I arrived late to practice one day and watched our unit try to march around the perimeter of the rectangular school-yard. Despite starting every practice of that first week with parade drilling, we had yet to complete an unbroken march around the yard. Our problem was not the length of the march; the playground was barely big enough for the pick-up baseball games played by the neighborhood's twelve- and thirteen-year-olds. Our problem was negotiating the three right-angle turns.

I watched my comrades trying their best to step in time, keep their shoulders back, swing their arms as one, and stop, turn, and restart in unison. But there was no synchrony to the movement of limbs. Nor was there uniformity in appearance. Everyone wore street clothes. There were almost as many women as men. And if most of my fellow militia members were in their early twenties, there were also a dozen teenagers and four or five people in their thirties and forties.

The drill instructor was working hard to keep everyone moving at the same speed and on the right line. I felt the strain of their effort. I saw the hope in their eyes when they negotiated the second turn. And I heard the collective groan when someone, halfway through the last one, made the in-evitable misstep that ruined the formation and set everyone to teasing him.

Every day of that first week we followed ten minutes of marching by taking turns sprinting twenty yards and hitting the ground ready to fire. We used wooden cutouts for rifles. We were supposed to sprint twenty yards and hit the ground, but almost everyone trotted to the spot, dropped to his or her knees, and plopped gently onto the grass before aiming the phony rifle.

Nobody went all out until the day I saw Ricardo watching from the edge of the schoolyard. I wanted to impress him. So I sprinted with my rifle and hit the ground running and assumed the firing position all in one motion—just like we were supposed to. One of the instructors yelled, "Yes! Finally! That's how to do it!"

But my moment of glory was brief. I had smacked my chin on the ground and bitten my tongue. I got up with watery eyes and spit out a reddish gob before wiping my mouth and smiling bravely. Everyone laughed. I looked at Ricardo. He was laughing too.

The best part of that first week was breaking into small groups every day to dig slit trenches in empty lots throughout the neighborhood. Everyone liked digging: the soil was loamy, we got to talk to each other, and unlike marching or hitting the ground with fake rifles, digging trenches made us feel as though we were actually accomplishing something.

Toward the end of that first week I found myself shoveling in a knee-deep trench when a forty-year-old woman whose teenage daughter was also in the militia asked me about Leon Trotsky. Her question was not altogether strange in revolutionary Nicaragua. Various neighbors and militia comrades had asked me to tell them about Karl Marx, the Soviet Union, and the differences between capitalism and socialism.

Just before going to Nicaragua I read a three-volume biography of Trotsky: *The Prophet Armed*, *The Prophet Unarmed*, and *The Prophet Outcast*. I liked Trotsky, mainly because he was the wildest and most brilliant of Marxist revolutionaries. He was a fiery speaker, he led the fight against counterrevolutionaries in Soviet Russia, he defended workers against party bureaucrats, he wrote about art and science, he was hounded out of Russia by Stalin, and he had a shock of black hair, a friend in Diego Rivera, and a lover in Frida Kahlo.

But I was no Trotskyite. I was no particular kind of Marxist at all. I was merely an academic Marxist from America pretending to be a revolutionary Marxist in Nicaragua. My Marxism was not political in any direct or meaningful way. I protested my government's policies in Central America, but I never fought for anything or organized a movement or joined the Socialist Workers Party. So I never developed "lines" about the various styles of guerrilla movements or revolutionary regimes in the Third World. I never even developed lines on the key issues facing the Sandinistas: whether to channel peasants into co-ops and collectives or give them plots of their own; when to hand over power to the workers and peasants; how to finish off an already wounded capitalist class; or what political role to assign the revolution's youth, students, and progressive sectors of the urban middle class.

Taking firm lines on the big issues would have turned me into a Leninist, a Trotskyite, a Maoist, a Fidelista, or a Guevarista, any one of which, in turn, would have turned me into a particular brand of Sandinista. But I was on the edge of the society and its revolution. I was more of a spectator than a participant. I cared more about being an American revolutionary than about the revolution itself. So I simply trusted that the comandantes and the rest of the Frente's vanguard intellectuals knew how best to lead the masses to socialism.

My political naiveté didn't stop me, however, from telling my militia comrades all about Trotsky. In fact, the very idea of giving a speech about Leon Trotsky while digging a trench in a working-class neighborhood played perfectly to my fantasy of being a revolutionary intellectual. While shoveling dirt and holding forth on the great Russian Marxist, I even imagined myself telling the story back home someday.

But as soon as I ended my ten-minute speech by saying that one of Stalin's agents had killed Trotsky in Mexico by plunging an ice axe into his head, the militiaman digging at the other end of the trench called me a liar. He accused me of "trying to confuse the people." He said I was a reactionary and an anticommunist. He then stated categorically that

Stalin had not ordered Trotsky's murder. "Yes he did," I said. "No he didn't," he replied.

Before I knew it, he had tossed aside his shovel and was coming toward me. He got right up into my face and demanded that I admit to lying about Stalin murdering Trotsky. I couldn't tell if he was in the Nicaraguan Communist Party, which followed Moscow, or if he was just badly confused or didn't like me for some reason. I stood my ground, threw my shovel aside, and said I was telling the truth.

So there we were, nose to nose and knee-deep in a trench and all ready to fight—over Stalin and Trotsky. My opponent was my age and my size, but he looked tougher than me. I noticed his muscular forearms. And I could see the fury in his eyes. I was scared, unsure of myself, and caught up in something I didn't understand. All of a sudden, the forty-year-old woman who had asked me about Trotsky stepped into the trench and got between us. I was relieved. I think he was too. From then on we stayed away from each other.

I was sure that Stalin had killed Trotsky. And I didn't mind getting into an argument. But the incident shook me up. It made me feel like an outsider who was messing around in someone else's business. My first real doubt about being in the militia had crept like a fog into the back of my mind.

The next day we arrived at the schoolyard to see three AK-47s and a dozen Czech VZ-52s laid out on the ground. We spent most of that second week taking them apart, putting them together, and learning how to set the sights and take aim while standing, kneeling, and lying down.

The rifles made me succumb entirely to the romance of training with a militia. And it *was* romantic to come home to an hour of rifle instruction after spending the day in the countryside doing social science for the revolution. I liked the image of myself as a pen-in-the-one-hand, rifle-in-the-other kind of revolutionary intellectual.

Toward the end of that second week of training, however, our lead instructor, Enrique, took me aside and asked, "Would you be willing to train as a sapper? It's a job for smart people. It will require extra instruction. We have to send one person from our unit for demolitions training."

As I looked at Enrique, who was five or six years older than I and had a wispy, Che-like beard, I saw images of fuses, wires, snippers, and plastic explosives, and I pictured things blowing up. For the first time, I recognized the obvious facts that being in the militia could mean fighting—and that fighting could mean killing.

Enrique surely saw my fear when I said, almost pleadingly, "I don't want to deal with explosives. I just want to be a regular foot soldier." I liked Enrique. He was quiet, confident, and relaxed, and he never lost patience with his inept trainees. I felt as though I was letting him down. But he touched me reassuringly on the shoulder and said, "Don't worry, it's not a problem."

While watching Enrique walk away I had a hopeful thought. The Frente, I said to myself, won't let an American fight anyway. Not a second later, I heard the word "hypocrite" in my head. But I heard it only once. And I immediately forgot it. Five minutes later I was taking apart an AK-47 as though nothing had happened.

15

We had not learned a thing about soldiering in two weeks of training, but we *had* learned to handle the rifles. And we were itching to use them. So we cheered when Enrique said we were going to the firing range early the next morning.

The excitement was palpable as we gathered in the schoolyard. The feeling grew steadily as we walked to a sand pit that had been turned into a shooting range. Our fervor reached its peak when we arrived to see that we had joined up with militia units from other parts of the neighborhood. A hundred and fifty militiamen in one spot, rifles and ammunition laid out on the ground, uniformed instructors carrying their AK-47s—the sight of all that made us feel powerful.

We were ordered to stand behind a row of two dozen rifles that had been laid out five feet apart. The corresponding targets were leaning against the base of a twenty-foot embankment. In between was a gently sloping plane of cream-colored sand.

Enrique was off to one side talking with his fellow instructors. They were gathered around the cocky Sandinista who had made me uneasy at the first meeting of our militia unit. While they talked I looked around and liked seeing that I was the only internationalist among so many Sandinistas.

A few minutes later, the cocky Sandinista stepped away from the instructors and came toward us. When he had our attention, he pulled his AK-47 off his shoulder and all in one motion fired a long, Rambo-like burst from his hip. The bullets hit a good ten or fifteen feet in front of the target, spraying it with an impressive shower of dirt. I saw Enrique shake his head.

But the embarrassing display did nothing to curb our excitement. And the instructors immediately called together their units, placed them at assigned spots along the row of rifles, and issued instructions.

Our first group of five got on the ground to shoot. I heard their rifles fire and saw puffs of sand fly off the dirt wall behind the targets some sixty or seventy yards away. My comrades were aiming high and shooting fast. They had shot their ten rounds before they knew it.

As I got on the ground to take my turn, I told myself to aim below the bull's-eye. I had shot a pellet gun as a kid but never a rifle. So I didn't know what to expect as I looked down the barrel of the gun, took aim, and steadied my finger on the trigger. I felt the soft recoil of the rifle against my shoulder and knew I had hit the target when no puff of sand flew off the wall. I took my time with the rest of my shots. I wanted to shoot well.

I never hit the bull's-eye, but hitting the target with every shot was good enough to give me the second-best score in our unit. When Enrique read out the top three scores and pronounced me as one of our snipers, someone yelled, "Hey me-cha-EL!"—which is how most Nicaraguans pronounced my name—"Maybe you'll be the first to kill a Yankee!"

We all laughed, but it was nervous laughter. I was nervous because shooting a rifle had just brought me one step closer to the reality of something I wasn't ready for: trying to shoot somebody. My comrades were nervous because shooting rifles had brought home the point that they, as the last line of defense against an American invasion, might actually have to try and kill Yankee soldiers—who knew how to kill a hell of a lot better than my comrades ever would.

Someone then asked, rhetorically, "What kind of Sandinista militia has a gringo sniper who can't hit the bull's-eye?" The answer was more nervous laughter. I then asked Enrique if we were coming back for more target practice. "I doubt it," he said.

16

The next morning I went to the telecommunications building to make my monthly call home. There was never much to discuss. My parents had no idea why I went to Nicaragua. Everything they knew about the place came from the nightly news, which only made them worry. They never asked what I was doing.

Despite taking a certain pleasure from their knowing that I was working for a revolution at war with our own government, I wanted my parents to know that I was safe. I always listened to my mother give me the news of my brothers before she handed the phone to my father, who didn't say anything. He simply listened to me talk for a minute or two about innocuous things like the wicked heat, the violent afternoon downpours, and a volcanic lagoon I had visited.

This time, however, I told my father that I was in a militia. I even told him that we had just taken target practice. I told him in order to show off, certainly. But I also told him because I was scared. He must have sensed my fear because he overcame his general reluctance to give advice of any kind. "Be careful," he said. "Don't let them brainwash you down there."

"Okay, Dad," I said with a laugh. "I'll call next month." I laughed off his remark, but it pestered me throughout the day.

I arrived home from the next day's training to find a boy of eleven or twelve waiting for me with a bag of bottle caps. He had seen me flick a few the day before, and I offered to give him a lesson if he brought me a bagful. The trick was to place the rim of the cap between your thumb and middle finger, hold your hand by your ear, point your elbow toward the target, adjust the angle of your wrist, and snap your fingers. I was good enough to hit the door of the house across the narrow street with every second or third shot.

A gaunt eighteen-year-old with bad skin came by while we were flicking the caps. I knew him by sight and reputation. Under circumstances that no one seemed sure about, the Sandinistas killed his older brother soon after taking power. Some people said the boy's family was counterrevolutionary. Everyone agreed that he had never gotten over his brother's death.

He watched silently for several minutes before saying, in an eerily calm voice, "The Sandinistas killed my brother for no reason." "I'm sorry about your brother," I said. "They're communists," he replied, "just like the Cubans."

I kept flicking caps and hoped he would go away, but a minute later he scolded me for joining the militia. "You're not just working for them any more," he said. "You're now a part of them. That's why I have to talk to you."

After telling the younger boy to run along, I asked the teenager to come inside. We stood face to face a few steps inside the open door. For ten minutes I tried rebutting, as calmly as I could, his repeated accusation that the Sandinistas were communist dictators. I admitted that the Sandinistas were socialists, but I tried to explain that they were democratic socialists trying to build a new society for all of Nicaragua's people. My vacuous comments only made him angrier. Eventually he raised his voice and said, "You're wrong! They killed my brother for nothing, just because he didn't like them. You've become one of them. You've joined their militia. You're going to fight for them."

While a part of me felt sorry for him, I couldn't see that he was just a disturbed kid looking for sympathy. Nor could I see that he had just hit a sore point by saying I was going to fight with the militia. A minute later we were yelling at each other.

At some point a gauzy red film dropped over my field of vision like a falling theater curtain. I rarely lost my temper. I certainly had never seen red. But I was suddenly looking at the frightened teenager through the reddish film and telling him that people on the wrong side of a just revolution deserve exactly what they get.

Everything stopped. He looked at me wide-eyed with disbelief. Tears rolled down his cheeks. As the red haze lifted from my field of vision, I put my hands on his shoulders, looked him in the eye, and said, "Your brother didn't deserve to die. I'm sorry for saying that. Please forgive me." He was too choked up to say anything, but he seemed to accept my apology with a nod of his head as he wiped his eyes with his sleeve. He let me guide him to the door.

I watched him walk away in the dusk, one elbow after the other flaring out from his shoulders as he kept wiping his eyes and nose with the back of his hands. He was wrong about the Sandinistas, I told myself, but I was wrong to argue with him. For a couple of seconds I wondered about his brother. Then I felt exactly like I had after arguing about Trotsky in the trench: as though I was getting involved in dangerous things that were no concern of mine.

*L*ate the next morning, Osvaldo and I went looking for "the patriotic bourgeoisie," a Sandinista euphemism for cowed and cooperative capitalists. The coffee harvest was about to begin, and I was ready to start counting the workers, but Osvaldo thought I could still learn something by talking to a couple of big coffee farmers. He had gotten their names from a friend who was a regional commander in Carazo. Osvaldo sometimes helped me with my fieldwork, but I was pretty sure that this time he just wanted to get away from the office for half a day, which was fine with me. Besides, I rarely got to ride in a ministry jeep. And the biggest capitalist I had met in Nicaragua owned a tiny restaurant in Managua.

The Carazo plateau is a hundred square miles of volcanic soil at fifteen hundred feet above sea level—perfect for growing coffee. Sporadic patches of corn, pasture, and woods break up the otherwise endless rows of coffee bushes. Dozens of tiny villages provide workers for the harvests, and several good-size towns live off the wealth generated by the coffee bean.

Osvaldo and I drove through an open gate and down a dirt driveway toward a large, two-story, whitewashed house that had been built when coffee was first planted in Carazo a century before. We got out of the jeep just as a man came out of the house. Before we had even shut our doors, Osvaldo yelled out that we were from the Agrarian Reform Ministry and wanted to ask the owner some questions. It was as though Osvaldo had identified himself as a detective in search of a suspect.

Michael Johns

The man seemed more irritated than worried. He was light-skinned, looked about thirty-five, and wore a thick mustache. He had the ruddy face of someone who worked outside.

Osvaldo stopped ten feet short of him before stating his name and introducing me as an American working for the ministry. The man looked at me as if to ask, "What the hell are *you* doing here?" He clearly wanted nothing to do with us, but he told us to come inside.

He called his wife into the living room and told her that we were Sandinistas who wanted to ask some questions. They sat down together on the couch. We sat in the chairs facing them. Osvaldo sat across from the farmer; I sat opposite his wife. There was a low serving table between us. Before proceeding with matters of any kind, Nicaraguans of every social class offer visitors something to drink or eat, if only water or the lowliest of sweets. But it was clear that nothing was about to be served on that table.

The living room had white stucco walls, a tile floor, and a high ceiling with exposed wood beams. The furniture was nice enough to make me self-conscious of my ratty sneakers and fraying jeans. Yet the place looked incomplete somehow, as if certain things had been removed. An empty space next to the staircase looked perfect for an armoire or a grand-father clock, and slight discolorations on the walls hinted where paintings might have hung. I wondered if the own-ers had removed certain items in fear of the country's new culture of class consciousness and revolutionary asceticism. Several comandantes had even issued a public warning of sorts: the wealth that used to be a sign of status, they said, was now a symbol of shame.

Osvaldo wasted no time. He didn't even explain the re-search we were doing. He simply told the farmer that we wanted to know where his harvesters came from, how many weeks they worked for him, and who arranged it.

"The number of harvesters varies from year to year," said the farmer. "They come here on their own and from all over the place, some as far away as Masaya. So I can't really help you." He sat very still and kept his hands flat on his thighs, but I could tell that he was fuming inwardly—about Osvaldo's insolence, about the invasive questions, about being questioned at all, especially in his own house.

I was acutely aware that we had all but trespassed on the farmer's property—and on his dignity as well. I could feel the power of the revolution behind us. And I liked it.

Osvaldo asked his questions again, and once more the farmer evaded them. But this time the farmer asked Osvaldo why he wanted to know about the workers. The farmer's question must have conjured up an unpleasant image in his own mind while he was in the very process of asking it, for he then asked, almost rhetorically and with a hint of fear in his voice, "What could you possibly want with that kind of information?"

The farmer had every reason to worry. While he could not have known that Osvaldo and I had no power to do anything or that the ministry had no immediate plans to take over the market for seasonal laborers, he knew all too well that the Frente taunted and vilified the upper classes all the time. He also knew that the Frente confiscated the property of those who criticized the revolution in front of their workers or failed to invest their capital in ways deemed appropriate by the ministry. The farmer must also have known that the very best he could hope for—should the Frente ultimately get its way—was to be a poor and pusillanimous capitalist controlled by Sandinista politicos and bureaucrats.

Instead of answering the farmer's question, Osvaldo warned him that refusing to cooperate could hurt his standing with the ministry. The farmer dug his fingers into his thighs and began to lean forward when his wife, who was sitting on the lip of the couch and looking back and forth between Osvaldo and her husband, put her hand on his knee.

He settled back and stared hard at Osvaldo. "Look," he said, "I'm middle-class just like you. I went to college just like you did. And like any number of the 'bourgeoisie,' as you like to call us, I backed the revolution against Somoza. All I want to do is make an honest living. I can't do that if you are going to take away my harvest workers and send them to the collective farms or have them make trouble for me."

I wasn't sure if he was needling Osvaldo about being a middle-class revolutionary or making a desperate appeal to some sense of class solidarity. But there was no mistaking the bad feeling between them.

Osvaldo stood up and said, "It's no use asking any more questions." I looked back and forth a few times between the couple, who stayed on the couch, and Osvaldo, who was walking toward the door. Only when he opened it and looked back at me did I get up and follow him out.

I was barely out of the house when the farmer opened the door and said, "Wait a second. Can I speak to you?" He was looking at me, not at Osvaldo, who was fifteen feet ahead. I looked back at Osvaldo, who frowned and shrugged as if to say, "It's a waste of time, but go ahead if you want to." So I went back inside.

The farmer shut the door, and he and his wife stood very close to me. "You're an American," he said, almost whispering. "Surely you understand that I need my property and my workers. I'm asking you not to let the Sandinistas take them from me." Speaking quickly now, he said that the Sandinistas were making it hard for him to stay in business and that he might have to sell his estate, like several other farmers he knew. He let me know that he, his wife, and their two teenagers had all grown up in Carazo and wanted to stay in Nicaragua. "And believe me," he said, "I'm no reactionary. I opposed Somoza and I supported the Sandinistas during their first year in power. But I can't support them any longer. They're ruining the country."

He stopped talking. They were staring at me, waiting for me to say that I could help them. I was suddenly aware that they were ten years older than I and running a coffee farm and raising children. I was suddenly aware, in other words, that they were mature adults while Osvaldo and I were something less than that. I came very close to apologizing for Osvaldo's bad manners and telling them that I understood their concerns about the revolution.

But I fought off my doubts. The farmer suddenly seemed pathetic to me for pleading his case like that—pathetic in a way that made me both pity him for his difficult situation and despise him for groveling. My contempt quickly overwhelmed my sympathy, however, and I began, quite unconsciously, to play a game with him.

I assured him that we were only doing a study. I told him that we had no plans to take away his workers or encourage the Rural Workers Union to make trouble for him. The Frente, I said, wanted to make sure that every coffee bean got harvested, for it needed the foreign exchange. I then told him that Osvaldo and I had no power to do anything—to him, to his farm, or to his workers.

So far as I knew, everything I said was true. But I said it with a certain hesitation and shiftiness so as to make him think that I was lying. I was trying to scare him, in other words, by making him think that I was reassuring him insincerely. I saw the confusion and fear on their faces and said I had to go.

I left in a daze. I didn't fully understand what I had just done, but I knew it was wrong. And I felt bad about it. As we drove away, I told Osvaldo only that the farmer had asked me not to take away his workers. "Think of the irony," he chuckled, "of a Nicaraguan capitalist asking a gringo Marxist to protect him from the Sandinista revolution." When I didn't laugh, Osvaldo knew something was wrong. And he knew what it was.

"Don't let it bother you," he said, beginning a little speech whose every word I hung onto as though they were guiding me back from the dangerous land of political doubts. "Every capitalist is chafing under the revolution, and this particular one tried to make you feel sorry for him. Even if he's a good guy, and I don't think he is, you can't think of him or of any other capitalist in personal terms. For even if they seem like nice guys and they tell you that they want to remain friendly with the revolution, they have a position in the class structure—they're capitalists after all!—which makes them, in the last instance, antagonistic to the economic needs of the workers and peasants and hostile to the political aspirations of the masses in general. You know perfectly well, Miguel, that these are structural contradictions, not personal failings on their part."

"So it naturally follows," he went on, "that even so-called patriotic bourgeoisie like our coffee farmer will use every opportunity to stall—and even overturn—the revolution. While it's true that most of the bourgeoisie opposed Somoza and a good many of them even helped to defeat him, they did so only because they wanted a reformed version of the old order—a kind of Somoza-ism without Somoza. But as we know, there is no reforming capitalism in any meaningful way. So the bourgeoisie will simply have to be pushed aside—slowly but surely—as the revolution advances. In the long run, of course, they will have to go away entirely as a class. That's all there is to it."

Osvaldo paused for a few seconds before saying, "So don't worry about the coffee farmer. He just wanted to make you feel bad for him and to make you doubt what you're doing."

By the end of Osvaldo's speech, I had moved the coffee farmer from the category of human being back into the category of bourgeoisie. And I felt ashamed for getting weak in the knees during my first encounter with a capitalist. I felt even worse for needing Osvaldo's help to restore my political courage. Yet I couldn't escape the now familiar feeling that I was getting deep into something that was not mine.

19

Only a week or two earlier, I was confidently discussing with Sergio and Osvaldo the theory that Nicaragua was in a state of what one of the comandantes called "revolutionary hegemony." I had impressed them by pointing out that the comandante's revolutionary hegemony was akin to Marx's "dictatorship of the proletariat," which Che had borrowed to describe Cuba in the early 1960s. Both phrases depict the initial stage in the transition to socialism. In this first phase, the vanguard uses its political power to weaken the biggest capitalists while inculcating the masses with a revolutionary consciousness.

Like everyone else at the Center, Sergio, Osvaldo, and I were sure that the revolution's hegemony was creating the initial conditions for making socialism in Nicaragua. Giving land to peasants, building labor unions, drawing citizens into revolutionary organizations, teaching poor people to read, providing electricity and water to slum dwellers, weakening the capitalist class—while every Sandinista supported those measures, no Sandinista saw them as ends in themselves. They were a means to the end of creating the new man and his new society.

There was only one fault in the logic of replacing capitalism with socialism: nobody had any idea what daily life in the socialist ideal was supposed to look like. The best we could do was to picture a cartoon version of the future in which everyone was more righteous and sincere, more libertine and carefree, more selfless and noble, more dedicated and responsible, more educated and skilled, more brotherly and sisterly, or more something or other depending on one's utopian inclinations. The cartoon is untrue to life and much duller besides: it is the future of an illusion.

So it's no wonder that Marx, Lenin, and Che failed to provide us with mental models of socialism. It's even less surprising that Cuba, China, and the USSR—which we called "actually existing" socialism in order to keep alive the hope of some future ideal of socialism—failed to provide us with real models. With no model of socialism, we had to rely on slogans—about eliminating exploitation and inequalities, about giving the means of production to the workers and peasants, about ending social classes and divisions of labor, about replacing private interests and private property with public interests and public property, about substituting co-operation for competition, about creating the new socialist man.

And when we couldn't visualize the slogans, we told ourselves that we didn't need a socialist blueprint anyway. It was enough, we said, to know that capitalism itself was the problem. From there it was simply a matter of placing our trust in *el proceso revolucionario*, the revolutionary process by which the dialectical interplay between the vanguard and the masses would discover the form of socialism that was appropriate to Nicaragua.

Our belief in the power of the revolutionary process to create socialism was based on our belief in the central tenet of Marxism: that there is no human nature or too little to matter. If you create the right conditions—co-operative and collective property, workers running their workplaces, a shared revolutionary outlook—you will eventually create the new man and his new society. The grand Marxian conceit, in other words, is that we humans can make our own history pretty much as we would like it to be. We simply need the political power to create the right economic and ideological conditions.

A lot of well-educated and otherwise intelligent people believed in that idea. We believed in it not because it made sense from our study of society or our experience of life. We believed in it because we needed what appeared to be a rational argument to sustain our faith in the revolution—and in the idea of ourselves as revolutionaries.

20

Enrique invited me to his home the night before our last day of training. He lived about ten blocks away with his wife and two little kids in a comfortable house with tile floors. In Managua, a family's floor was a good indicator of its class: dirt was for the bottom half, cement the next third, and tile or wood the top sixth.

A day or two earlier Enrique and I had gone out for tacos after practice. I told him about my study. He described the program he ran for training teachers at the Ministry of Education. And we talked about baseball, which American Marines had introduced to Nicaraguans in the 1910s. We even decided to see an upcoming game between two of Managua's best teams. Not once, though, did we discuss the revolution, our militia, or the odds of an American invasion.

So I was taken by surprise when Enrique began criticizing the Frente after we had drunk five or six glasses of rum and just finished a conversation about jazz while listening to a John Coltrane album in his living room, which was furnished with a set of low, angular, slender-legged modernist furniture from the 1960s. The only sign of Nicaragua's revolution was a kerchief-sized red and black flag—the FSLN banner—tacked to a shelf on a small bookcase. I imagined Enrique wearing it around his neck while fighting Somoza's National Guardsmen some four and a half years earlier.

"Have you ever noticed," he said, straight out of nowhere, "that for all the talk about a 'dialectical' relationship between the vanguard and the masses"—Enrique fingered a pair of quote marks around the word dialectical—"the system is pure *verticalismo*?" He saw my confusion. "Well, it's true," he said. "The comandantes simply *bajan lineas* so as to give everyone their *orientación*."

He described the top-down process by which the comandantes "dropped lines" of orientation through the tiers of revolutionary organizations—through the tiers of Sandinista ministries, the Sandinista army, the Sandinista militias, the Sandinista Defense Committees, the Sandinista Youth, the Sandinista labor unions, the Sandinista women's organization, the Sandinista teachers association, and, of course, through the tiers of the Frente Sandinista itself, the self-described Vanguard Party of the Revolution. The lines eventually reached local-level leaders and cadres who, in turn, passed them on to rank-and-file supporters of the revolution. "Nine out of ten Sandinistas don't think," said Enrique. "They get oriented by the lines that come down to them from on high."

Enrique went on to complain that the comandantes had never held a party congress or a party election, not even since taking power. "They act like they own the Frente," he said. "I respect the comandantes for all they've done, but only a couple of them were even in the country during the last five or six years of the dictatorship. And they didn't get along among themselves or constitute a coherent group until a few months before the final insurrection against Somoza, in which they played hardly any role. Only one of them, you know, did any fighting. Yet they think the revolution belongs to them—personally. Let me tell you something: the comandantes will always be the vanguard. They like to say that it's a people's revolution; that they, the comandantes, simply put into action the wishes of the masses; that the workers and peasants will someday be in charge. Well, believe me when I tell you that the revolution will always belong to the comandantes. They will always be in charge. So much for 'democratic' socialism." Again he made quote marks with his fingers.

Despite some erosion in my certainty about the revolution, I was not at all prepared to see the obvious truth that the Frente was hierarchical and authoritarian. I was not even willing to view the comandantes as anything less than Nicaraguan versions of Che Guevara. I certainly did not like hearing the revolution criticized by someone whose ideas I could not dismiss.

So I tried to halt the barrage of uncomfortable facts by filling a pause in Enrique's criticism with an imprudent joke. "You're an oxymoron, Enrique: a reactionary revolutionary!" He looked at me hard and said, "You like being in the militia, huh? You think you're a revolutionary? Well you're nothing but a *rábano* [radish]." He saw my confusion, so he spelled it out. "Politically speaking, you're red on the outside but white on the inside."

When he saw my confusion turn to fear, he knew that he had gone too far. It was too late for him to retract his words about the Frente, words he had spoken with the help of rum and out of the misplaced hope that I would understand them. But he still had a chance to take back what he had just said about me. So he forced a smile and said, "I was only kidding about you being a radish, just like you were kidding about me being a reactionary revolutionary."

I had to believe him. There was no other way to deal with his calling me a rábano. He poured another drink and said, "All right, all right, enough about the revolution for one night." I was already forgetting that he had called the comandantes little dictators—and that he had called me a radish.

21

I walked into the schoolyard and saw Enrique talking to the Sandinista who spoke to us on our first day of training and then shot from the hip, quite literally, at the firing range. He must have come to make a final inspection. A few minutes later he ordered us to follow him around the block. We all looked at Enrique, who nodded.

The visiting Sandinista started yelling "¡No pasarán!" as soon as we entered the street. We took up his chant and shouted it for a block. Then he switched us to "¡El pueblo, unido, jamás será vencido!" This is the one slogan whose English translation—"The people, united, will never be defeated!"—keeps the exact Spanish rhythm. By next chanting "¡Alerta! ¡Alerta! ¡La lucha guerrillera por América Latina!" we alerted everyone on the third block to the coming guerrilla struggle for the control of Latin America.

But none of us chanted passionately. We didn't like it that the visitor had taken over from Enrique. And most of us felt sheepish besides. Even in a country run by revolutionaries, you need a lot more than thirty people to feel confident and powerful yelling slogans through the narrow streets of your own neighborhood.

As we approached the final corner, our visitor turned around and yelled, "¡Aquí, allá, el yanki morirá!" I had never heard it before. It means something like "Here, there, and everywhere, all the Yankees will die." At first only five or six militiamen chanted with him. Everyone else seemed to be looking at me to see if I would wish death upon my countrymen.

A few seconds later, I did. And as soon as I yelled the slogan, everyone else did too. Several people caught my eye and smiled. All at once we were screaming the hard-cadenced slogan at the top of our lungs. It was as though we dealt with its apparent threat to me by whipping ourselves into a near-frenzy over it.

Seven or eight people gathered immediately around me when we entered the schoolyard. They apologized for the slogan. A few declared their fondness for Americans. Somebody said, "You're not a Yankee. Yankees are imperialists. You're an internacionalista." Even Enrique came over to pat me on the shoulder and tell me not to worry about it.

Then he ordered us to line up for parade marching. We groaned. We hated marching. We were no good at it. We had not done it for almost two weeks. And we knew that Enrique was ordering us to march only because our uninvited guest had told him to.

Halfway around the schoolyard I had the crystal-clear thought that I was never going to shoot at anybody—especially a U.S. Marine. In fact, I was absolutely sure that I would try to leave the country if we got credible warnings of an imminent U.S. invasion. Worst of all, I pictured myself running to the American embassy should the United States invade before I could get out.

A moment later I had my one and only out-of-body experience: I saw myself marching as a fraudulent militiaman. I snapped out of it when someone ahead of me took a wrong step at the third turn and broke up the formation. We quickly regrouped and marched the last fifty yards.

All I could think about for the rest of that last practice was having to tell Enrique I was leaving the militia—and having Elena, Ricardo, and my militia comrades find out that I was a coward and a quitter. I was especially worried about Soraya's finding out.

Soraya and I met three months earlier while helping our Defense Committee paint a small elementary school in the neighborhood. We had been sleeping together since. We didn't have a relationship; we had sex. Soraya had dark eyes, perfect brown skin, and waves of thick, black hair that fell below her shoulders. She was irresistible when the muggy weather dotted her upper lip with tiny beads of sweat and inflated her hair into a bouncy mass of curls. And she liked showing off her twenty-year-old body as much as I liked looking at it. Once, after we had made love on the mattress in my tiny bedroom, she got up, took a few steps back, and did several slow twirls with outstretched arms so I could admire her. Then she cupped her breasts and said, "You should have seen these when I was fifteen—they kissed the sky!"

Soraya was pert and cute, but what I liked best about her was that she was a Sandinista barrio girl. Soraya had only eight years of schooling. She lived with her mother and two younger sisters in a one-room shack. She belonged to the Sandinista Youth. And she worked in a collective bakery. Sleeping with a Sandinista girl from a working-class neighborhood played perfectly into my sense of myself as an American revolutionary.

The truth, however, is that I didn't really like Soraya as a Sandinista barrio girl. I liked the *idea* of Soraya as a Sandinista barrio girl. We never once talked about the revolution. I was afraid of her ideas because I suspected they were even vaguer than those of the Sandinista youths with whom I was reading the *Primer on Marxism*. And apart from painting the school, we never worked together on any revolutionary projects. I knew that we had almost nothing in common.

Yet I clung to the idea that she was the real thing, the lower-class Sandinista. And I indulged the idea that we were both working for this grand thing called La Revolución. The two ideas combined to spark the sexual connection in the first place, and they made it feel deeper than it was and last longer than it otherwise would have.

The affair worked because we only had time for sex. I was in Carazo or Masaya several days a week, and Soraya was working long hours at the bakery and spending many of her evenings and most of her weekends doing some kind of revolutionary activity with her Youth Brigade. Neither of us had phones, so she just dropped by when she could. One of my favorite memories of Nicaragua is coming home late at night from a day of fieldwork to find Soraya waiting for me in my bed.

So of course I was wondering, as we ran through our last militia drills, whether my affair with a Sandinista barrio girl was about to end.

22

"You don't have to quit," said Enrique, somehow anticipating what I was going to say. We were standing in the dusk at the entrance to the schoolyard where I had waited for everyone to leave so I could talk to him alone. "Just forget about the whole thing. We're done training. And unless the Americans invade, and I don't think they will, the militia will never meet up again anyway. So don't worry about it." I was incredibly relieved that I didn't have to quit and that nobody but Enrique would know that I had wanted to.

"But I do have to tell you," he said, "that you joined the militia for selfish reasons. And you mocked the sincerity of your compañeros, who joined with the full intention of doing their best to defend their country."

I didn't understand what Enrique meant by "selfish reasons," for I hadn't the faintest idea that I had joined the militia mainly to live up to an image of myself as some kind of revolutionary intellectual. Nor did I understand how I had mocked the sincerity of my comrades. But I definitely felt the sting of his words. For there was no denying the main fact: I had joined a militia that I was not willing to fight with. And I was ashamed of myself.

After staring at me for several long seconds, as if to make sure I felt the heat of the moment, he softened his tone and said, very deliberately, so as to make sure I understood him fully, "Forget about the militia. You never should have joined in the first place. The revolution needs your brains, not your brawn. Leave the fighting to us. It's our country and our revolution, not yours. It's our war to fight, not yours. Do you understand? You have no duty to fight for this revolution. In fact, it would be stupid for you do to so. Believe me, you're already doing plenty for the revolution with your study. You're doing much more than most Nicaraguans are doing and more even than many Sandinistas are doing. So keep focused on your work. Dedicate all of your energy to it. It's important."

He finished his short speech by saying, "Look, we truly appreciate what internationalists like you are doing for us. You're not like those fucking Sandalistas who come here wanting to be revolutionary tourists for ten days so they can return home telling everyone about their revolutionary experience."

I had never heard the word "Sandalistas." Nor had I met any of them. But I knew that Enrique was talking about the self-styled "brigades" of American and European sympathizers who came to Nicaragua for a couple of weeks to "help" the revolution. I laughed at the clever epithet: Sandal-ista. He laughed too. And with that we hugged each other and said good-bye. I knew that I would never see him again.

I went home feeling grateful to Enrique, though I didn't fully comprehend what he had just done for me. Some part of him surely wanted me to see the revolution as he saw it—and to see myself as the radish he knew me to be. Yet he decided to let me figure it out on my own. Perhaps he wanted no responsibility for making me lose faith in the revolution. Maybe he lacked the patience to educate a callow American who wasn't ready to think critically about himself and the world around him. It's even possible that Enrique felt vulnerable after revealing his doubts about the revolution—doubts that I barely comprehended, let alone appreciated for their power to mess up his life as a Sandinista.

For whatever reasons, Enrique let me ignore some very uncomfortable facts. And in so doing, he let me hold on to my image of myself as an American revolutionary in Sandinista Nicaragua—for a few more weeks, anyway, until I met a group of the Sandalistas he had made fun of.

23

The first Sandalista I saw had the sticker "I'd Rather be Smashing Imperialism" on his backpack. Several others wore T-shirts bearing images of Che Guevara or slogans like "U.S. out of El Salvador." A middle-aged woman with a red beret was showing off a piece of revolutionary art she had bought. Her small watercolor on plywood depicted peasants working the fields with rifles slung over their shoulders and red and black bandanas tied around their necks. But most of the fifty or sixty Sandalistas I saw that afternoon showed no outward signs of their revolutionary sympathies. They looked like they could have belonged to any random group of white, college-educated Americans between the ages of twenty-five and fifty-five.

This particular group of Sandalistas was part of the first international work brigade to visit Nicaragua. Dozens of small cultural brigades had come from the United States and South America to teach dance and theater or paint murals on buildings. Delegations of left-wing union members from Canada and the United States had come to meet cadres from the Rural Workers Union and the Sandinista Workers Federation. Believers in liberation theology had come to "stand witness" to contra incursions along the northern border with Honduras.

But this international work brigade was special. Its three or four hundred volunteers made it the single largest group of foreign sympathizers to visit the revolution. Its members would be the first foreigners to spend two weeks harvesting coffee on Sandinista farms. And they would be working un-

Michael Johns

der the threat of an expected American assault on Nicaragua. For all those reasons, the Frente got actively involved, for the first time, in arranging the experiences of visiting sympathizers.

I learned about the brigade through an American doctoral student who worked at the Center. He was helping the Frente organize the arrival of one of the American contingents. So he asked me and another resident American to help him welcome our compatriots at a rustic conference center on the outskirts of Managua.

On the afternoon of their arrival the Sandalistas heard two talks under a thatched roof in a courtyard. The first was by a white-haired Sandinista general. He wore a uniform and carried a side arm, but he looked much too old to have fought in the insurrection against Somoza.

I was watching from behind and to one side of him as he stared at his audience for several seconds before removing his pistol from its holster, holding it up for everyone to see, and carefully placing it on the table in front of him. He then leaned over and slowly slid the gun—ultimately using the fingertips of his outstretched arm—to the far edge of the table. And there it lay—just beyond his immediate reach.

He let his gesture sink in before sitting down and saying, through a translator, "You see? I am here with Americans who have a revolutionary consciousness and represent the best spirit of your people, not the imperialist attitude of your government. So I don't need the gun. Nor do I fear that anyone here will want to use it against me."

I smiled at what seemed like the calculated absurdity of a fawning gesture. But he didn't smile or say anything to indicate that he was joking. And the Sandalistas seemed genuinely impressed by it. So I had no idea whether he meant his gesture seriously or was mocking the gullibility of the Sandalistas or was indeed trying to make a joke but was himself surprised when the nickel failed to drop in the brains of his audience.

The old general spoke for only a few minutes before giv-

ing way to a twenty-five-year-old Sandinista wearing khakis
and a nice button-down shirt. The young Sandinista gave us a
glossy overview of the revolution in perfect English. He cited
figures on the transfer of land to peasants, he extolled the
widespread participation of the Nicaraguan people in revolutionary organizations, and he praised the literacy campaign
that had been carried out by Sandinista Youth during the first
year of the revolution. He assured us that the Frente wanted
a mixed economy and would continue to respect the property rights of each and every landowner who was willing to
work with the people. He also affirmed the revolution's commitment to political pluralism and free speech. The Frente,
he went on to explain, censored the opposition newspaper,
La Prensa, only when it sided with the counterrevolution.

While the Frente was not a Marxist or a Leninist party, Nicaragua was now an open country, he said, whose people were
free to engage with Marxism or any other kind of thought.
After admitting that the Frente made a mistake in trying to
relocate thousands of Miskito Indians on the Atlantic Coast,
he blamed the CIA and the contras for creating the problems
in the first place. Although several thousand Cubans were
working in Nicaragua as doctors, engineers, and teachers, so
too, he added, were there Swiss doctors, French engineers,
and Canadian teachers. And even though the comandantes
were at odds with Nicaragua's archbishop, the problem was
political, he said, not religious: the archbishop was siding
with the counterrevolution. To prove his point, the Frente's
young spokesman gave the examples of the minister of culture, who was a Jesuit, and the foreign minister, who was
a Maryknoll priest. He then quoted a line from one of the
Frente's literacy primers—"There is freedom of religion for
every church supporting the people."

He finished his talk by denying the Reagan administration's accusation—which I knew to be correct—that the
Frente was sending arms to revolutionaries in El Salvador.
He drew a rough map of Nicaragua, Honduras, and El Salvador and then laughed off the possibility of sending arms

through southwestern Honduras, where contras and Hondu-
ran soldiers watched the border, or by boat or plane across
the Gulf of Fonseca, which was patrolled by American ships
and planes. While the Frente was proud to give moral and
diplomatic support to its revolutionary brothers in El Salvador, he said, it had never sent them arms.

All at once I realized that he was using a mix of facts, lies,
and half-truths to create a superficial picture of the revolution for what the Frente assumed were badly informed and
guilt-ridden liberals. For a moment I felt sorry for the Sandalistas. They had come all the way to Nicaragua, I thought,
and at least they deserved to hear the Frente's honest view
of its own revolution. Then I remembered Trotsky saying, in
his book *Literature and Revolution*, that "fellow-travellers" are
not Marxists. So they fail to "grasp the Revolution as a whole
and the Communist ideal is foreign to them. . . . As regards
a 'fellow-traveller,' the question always comes up—how far
will he go?"

That's when I understood that the Frente's spokesman
was giving the Sandalistas exactly what they wanted—and
all that they could handle, politically speaking. Like Trotsky
said, you never know how far they will go. I then looked at
them in the condescending way that Marxists looked at liberals. They didn't really understand that this was a revolutionary transition to socialism, I said to myself, but at least
they had anti-imperialist instincts. And their instincts would
improve in Nicaragua and help them better defend the revolution back home.

24

Strips of sunlight cut through the wispy shade trees; rows of coffee bushes defied the mountain slopes like a street grid laid upon a hilly city; patches of sapphire sky, strips of black soil, and clusters of red beans offset the great green mass of shiny leaves: it was a lovely place to work. And the work was easy. You had only to reach out your arms, pick the marble-sized beans from their slender branches, drop them into the wicker basket tied around your waist, and empty the basket now and again into one of the big gunnysacks spaced throughout the grove. I especially liked the quiet and privacy afforded by the head-tall coffee bushes and the canopy of shade trees.

The Sandalistas had already gone into the groves and fanned out for their first day of work by the time I and the two Americans from the ministry arrived at the collective farm to join our compatriots for a day or two of coffee picking. So I scarcely saw the Sandalistas until we were called out of the fields to eat lunch in a grassy clearing. Our food was brought out from the main compound on the back of an old pickup truck. Two plump Nicaraguan women in sundresses scooped plastic cups of sweet black coffee from a big blue pot and handed out thick tortillas that they loaded with rice and beans ladled from a wooden box the size of a footlocker.

I was in line behind two American women in their late thirties. They wore jeans, sneakers, long-sleeved shirts, and baseball hats. One of them was praising Venezuela and Mexico for supplying Nicaragua with cheap oil since *el triunfo*. She said *el triunfo*—which is how Sandinistas referred to their overthrow of Somoza—as casually as if she had said "the triumph" or "the victory" in English. And she used an exaggerated Spanish accent to pronounce Nicaragua as NEE-kuh-RAH-gwuh. Yet she pronounced Mexico and Venezuela as would any other American who spoke no Spanish.

I didn't cringe, however, until they both said, "Gracias compa" (Thanks, comrade), to the two Nicaraguan women who had just served them their coffee and tortillas. The Nicaraguan women smiled politely and said, "De nada" (You're welcome). I felt compelled to make small talk with the Nicaraguans just to show them that I actually spoke Spanish and did not call strangers *compa*, revolutionary slang for *compañero*. I ate quickly and went back to the groves, where it was easy to avoid the Sandalistas for the rest of the afternoon.

25

We ate our supper of rice, beans, and tortillas while watching a skit performed on a makeshift stage in the mess hall. The actors were part of a large group of Sandinista Youth who were staying at the collective farm to harvest coffee. The skit was a dance in mime. An evil-looking Uncle Sam stood in the background directing contra attacks against innocent campesinos on an agricultural co-operative. Eventually, Sandinista soldiers came to teach the campesinos to defend themselves. The peasants were soon working the fields with rifles on their backs. They repulsed the next attack and sent the contras and Uncle Sam scurrying back to their haven in Honduras. Now the campesinos could get on with their main job, which was spelled out for them on a banner stretching across the entrance to their co-op: Producir para el Pueblo (To Produce for the People).

After the skit, the Sandalistas and Sandinistas got to know each other—as best they could, anyway, given that so few Americans knew Spanish and even fewer Nicaraguans knew English. In one corner of the mess hall a dozen Americans had gathered around a young Nicaraguan with a guitar. They understood each other well enough so that when he played "Fusil contra fusil" (Rifle against Rifle)—a revolutionary song written in homage to Che Guevara—the Sandalistas were able to follow his cue to chime in with the three words of the title that made up the chorus. They sang the song four or five times before trying another.

At the other end of the mess hall a group of Americans was listening to several Sandinista youths taking turns reading poems. One of the Americans knew enough Spanish to render the essence of the short poems to his compatriots. The poems were read from *Poesía de la Nueva Nicaragua*, an anthology of poems that had been published in the journal *Poesía Libre*. The journal was put out by the Culture Ministry, whose purpose, according to the man who ran it, was "to turn Nicaraguan culture into a wholly revolutionary culture."

Creating a revolutionary culture is hard under the best of circumstances, and Nicaragua's were not all that good. The Culture Ministry lacked the talent and money to make movies or television programs. Its two new museums, the Museum of the Revolution and the Museum of Literacy, consisted of propagandistic displays that attracted few (and mostly foreign) visitors. Baseball was popular but hard to invest with political meaning. And nothing could stop Nicaragua's youth—not even its Sandinista Youth—from preferring Michael Jackson's "Billie Jean" and "Beat It" to revolutionary songs like "A Hymn to Literacy" and "Together We'll Overcome Our Ignorance."

But the Culture Ministry did have an excellent resource: Nicaraguans' love and talent for poetry. Starting with Rubén Darío in the late 1800s, Nicaragua developed a continuous line of very good poets. The newspaper *La Prensa* had a long tradition of publishing the poems of its citizens. And several top Sandinistas were better suited for writing poetry than leading a revolution. So the Culture Ministry held poetry workshops all over the country and published the best results in the journal it created precisely for that purpose.

Back in Managua, I had my own copy of *Poesía de la Nueva Nicaragua*. So I recognized the poems read aloud in the mess hall that evening. One of them was "Love between Reservists":

Mariel
Let me start kissing your cheeks
your lips
your body.

For it could be too late tomorrow:
the Yankee Marines might be here.
Then we won't be together any longer.
You'll be patching up wounded comrades
behind the lines
and I'll be in the line of fire.

I liked the poem. I liked the skit, too. I especially liked "Rifle against Rifle" and knew it by heart. I liked them not because they were good examples of poetry, theater, or song writing but because, as a young Marxist supporting a transition to socialism, I agreed with the culture minister: "The role of culture in the new Nicaragua," he wrote in an essay called "Cultura revolucionaria," "is to develop a revolutionary consciousness among the people and help them make economic transformations."

While looking around the mess hall, however, I didn't like seeing the Sandalistas taking part in the revolutionary culture of the new Nicaragua. In fact, I didn't like the Sandalistas at all. I could not stop thinking that they wanted an instant connection to a revolution they knew nothing about. I looked down on them for coming to Nicaragua on a group tour rather than on their own. And I felt downright contemptuous when it dawned on me that they had not even come to pick coffee for the revolution.

As inexperienced harvesters, they would not be able to pick enough coffee in two weeks to cover the cost of the rice, beans, and tortillas they were eating, never mind the cost of transporting them to and from the collective farm in a rugged and isolated part of northern Nicaragua. The Sandalistas had come instead to harvest what Enrique called a "revolutionary experience." And the Frente was happy to provide it—so its American sympathizers would go home more committed than ever to stopping their imperialist government from harassing the revolution.

26

While I was trying to suppress my uncharitable thoughts about the Sandalistas, someone told me that Phil Agee was at the farm. I knew that Agee was the ex-CIA agent who wrote *Inside the Company: CIA Diary*. In addition to recounting his classified work with the CIA, Agee named dozens of agents and gave secret information to the Cubans. The American government revoked his passport, and he was deported from three or four countries in western Europe. He lived in Hamburg and traveled regularly to Cuba and Grenada, whose revolutionary governments had granted him citizenship. Just three or four months earlier Agee had visited Managua to discuss the CIA's counterrevolutionary tactics with the Interior Ministry. The ministry then gave him a passport when the United States invaded Grenada.

I was eager to meet him—and get away from the Sandalistas. I found his bunkhouse among the two dozen or so that were in the clearing behind the mess hall. I stood in the open doorway and saw four middle-aged men in the candlelight. They were sitting on the two lower bunk beds. I identified myself as an American working for the Agrarian Reform Ministry and said I was looking for Phil Agee. He invited me in. I sat on the floor between the bunks with my back against the wall. Agee passed the bottle of rum. He had wide, narrow eyes, a square chin, thin lips, and a long, straight mouth. His face reminded me of a Frank Lloyd Wright building: everything oriented toward the horizontal.

I was taking my first swig when Agee asked about the Frente's co-operatives and collectives. I had visited at least a dozen of them in Carazo and Masaya, but I knew almost nothing about how they actually worked. So I gave Agee the standard account of the several kinds of Sandinista farms, and I provided some numbers about their acreage, membership, and relative weight in the economy.

He seemed interested, but I feared that I was telling him what he already knew. And I wanted badly to impress him with my inside knowledge of the agrarian reform. So I revealed a disquieting and poorly known fact: the Frente's co-ops and collectives were all in debt despite getting government loans at negative interest rates. But there was no need to worry, I said. This is still the first phase of the agrarian reform, and the Frente's main goal is to raise the revolutionary consciousness of the peasants. Raising the productivity of their labor will come later, I said. I had no idea what I was talking about. I probably didn't even believe it. But I bolstered my argument by quoting a line I had heard from the manager of a collective farm in Carazo: "We didn't make a revolution to be slaves to capitalist notions of productivity and profit." Agee nodded in agreement. One of his companions said, "That's right." I knew they were impressed.

I was even more pleased with myself when Agee said that CIA agents working out of the U.S. embassy in Managua were surely watching me. And if the FBI didn't already have a file on me, he said, it would start one when I got home. Even the IRS would be after me. It felt as though Agee was paying me a compliment.

I secretly liked the idea of being watched by my government. I had enjoyed thinking, for example, that the FBI was taking pictures at our campus rallies. And like my left-wing friends, I regularly threatened to use the Freedom of Information Act to request my FBI file. But none of us did. We were afraid, I think, to find out that there were no files on us. We enjoyed our fantasies of political persecution only because, in contrast to Chilean, Argentine, Uruguayan, Guatemalan, or Salvadoran left-wingers, we had no real fear that anyone in our government would harm us.

At some point in the conversation Agee said he wanted to go to one of the weekly "vigils" that foreign residents had been holding in front of the U.S. embassy in Managua since the invasion of Grenada. I had gone to one. I arrived late and saw fifteen or twenty people waving placards and shouting slogans in a small circle in front of the high-gated entrance to the embassy. As I got closer, they stopped marching to arrange themselves in a semicircle around a young woman with a guitar. She stood with her back to the gate. From twenty or thirty yards away I watched them sing a revolutionary song by Nicaragua's Carlos Mejía Godoy. He was a low-grade version of Cuba's Silvio Rodríguez, who wrote "Rifle against Rifle." Somebody then gave a testimonial, a short speech about a personal experience meant to commend the revolution and condemn the United States. That's when I left. I shared the cause of my fellow internationalists, but I didn't like giving testimonials, singing songs, or yelling slogans.

So I was surprised when Agee said he wanted to attend a vigil in order to give a testimonial. He probably wants to have some fun with his former employer, I thought to myself. But then he said, "After what happened in Grenada, I have decided to live the rest of my life fighting imperialism and supporting the causes of Cuba, Nicaragua, and revolutionary movements everywhere."

The serenity with which he stated his conviction scared me. When I saw the depth of belief in his eyes, I knew that I had nowhere near his level of commitment. I suddenly understood why a fifty-year-old man with so much experience and knowledge of the wider world would be picking coffee with Sandalistas on a collective farm in a remote corner of northern Nicaragua. I said good night a few minutes later.

I didn't like seeing Agee as a fanatic. I didn't like seeing the Sandalistas as revolutionary tourists, either. What I liked least of all, however, was knowing, if only in the recesses of my mind, that I was seeing a part of myself in all of them.

Gunfire erupted all around us at three in the morning. I dropped down from the top bunk and crawled outside behind my two fellow internationalists. We lay on the ground listening to what must have been a half minute of sustained shooting. The next thing we heard was a Sandinista telling everyone that it was just nervous militiamen firing into the night. Then we heard a Sandalista saying she had enough Valium for anyone who needed it.

Three hours later nobody looked excited about picking coffee for the revolution. We had barely slept since the gunfire. We ached from the bare wooden bunks. We bled from scratching bug and spider bites on our ankles, necks, and forearms. We were sick of rice and beans and tortillas. And I was tired of the Sandalistas.

I couldn't tell my colleagues from the ministry that I couldn't stand our compatriots. I could barely admit it to myself. So I was pleasantly surprised when they suggested that we spend the day visiting a couple of nearby towns instead of picking coffee.

The Sandinista in charge of protecting the farm insisted we carry guns. He reminded us that we were only ten miles from Honduras, where the contras had their base camps. And he told us that a gang of contras had killed several people at the farm two months earlier. But he didn't have to convince us to take AK-47s and pistols; the thrill of carrying guns was much greater than the chance of running into counterrevolutionaries.

Even after failing as a Sandinista militiaman, I still wanted to see myself as an American revolutionary. I wanted the Sandalistas to see me that way, too. So although I knew better than to be seen with a rifle, I made sure to carry my AK-47 right past a small group of them on my way to the car.

Taking guns in the car was stupid. We barely knew how to shoot them, and we had no idea how to fight with them. So they only increased our chances of getting killed. At one point along the twisty mountain road I realized that it would be nearly impossible to fire my AK-47 from the front passenger seat in the case of an ambush. And if contras had managed to stop the car and disarm us without firing a shot, which is almost certainly what would have happened if we had run into them, we would have been in big trouble for carrying Sandinista weapons. But we weren't thinking; we were pretending to be revolutionaries.

Even stupider than taking guns in the car was carrying them on foot through a dusty backwoods town where half of the people hated the Sandinistas. San Juan de Limay sat in a long valley framed by rugged hills where Sandinista soldiers chased counterrevolutionaries. The contras tended to ambush vehicles and raid collective farms, but every so often they walked right into towns like Limay to burn government buildings and kill Sandinista officials.

Yet we blithely carried the guns through the town's dirt streets. We passed men on horseback. We walked by the open doors of a grocery store and a tortilla maker. And we saw a butcher draping long, thin strips of salted beef across what looked like a hitching post where they would dry in the sun. We were looking for a Sandinista co-operative. Its artisans carved figurines from white and pink soapstone found in local streams. The Culture Ministry was trying to help the artisans market their products to revolutionary tourists in Managua. We eventually found the co-op, but it was closed.

Later that afternoon, we got out of the car to photograph ourselves with the guns. The pocket camera was mine. So was the idea of taking the pictures. I didn't like taking photographs, and I hated posing for them. I took the camera to Nicaragua only because a friend had given it to me specifically for my trip. And I had it with me that day only because going to the coffee farm seemed like a vacation. The three photos I took along the road that afternoon were the first in the only roll of film I shot in Nicaragua. So I really wanted that picture of myself with an AK-47—even in a mock pose as a menacing revolutionary.

28

Back at the farm that evening a cute Sandalista about my age mistook me for a Sandinista. She must have seen me carrying the rifle or heard me talking to Nicaraguans. She introduced herself to me with very bad Spanish when I was coming out of the kitchen with a cup of coffee. I played along. We sat facing each other on a bench in a corner of the nearly empty mess hall. Most of the other coffee pickers had retired to their bunkhouses.

I was able to understand her only because I had spoken equally bad Spanish when I went to Mexico two and half years before. It also helped that I knew exactly what she was trying to tell me—that she admired the Sandinistas, hated Ronald Reagan, and thought the United States could learn a lot from Nicaragua's revolution.

Before long we were flirting, though I knew perfectly well that she was flirting not with me but with her impression of me as a Sandinista. Still, I liked the flirtation itself as much as I liked leading her on. And the game became harder to stop with every smile, touch of the knees, and locking of our eyes for just a second too long.

At some point she reached out and gently touched a nasty-looking scar on the side of my neck where I had been scraped by a branch while walking through some woods in Carazo a few weeks earlier. "¡Qué malo!" (How bad!), she said. "¿Cómo?" (How?), she asked. I answered with simple words and a lot of gestures to make sure she understood that I had been grazed by a contra's bullet.

She nearly swooned. I knew right then that it was time to stop the charade. "I'm only kidding," I said in English. "I wasn't shot." She looked puzzled. "How do you know English?" "I'm from Massachusetts." I saw the light go on behind her eyes before she hissed "Asshole!" and walked away.

I still felt like an asshole when I lay down to sleep an hour later. But I was glad to know that we would be leaving the Sandalistas for good in the morning.

29

The ministry's version of a personnel manager was tiny. Her fatigues and side arm made her look even smaller. And when she pulled her soft military cap over her curly mass of light-brown hair, she reminded me of Bozo the Clown. But she had a big job: vetting everyone who wanted to work for the ministry or at the Center and making sure they followed the Frente's line once they got there.

Right after I moved into the office with Sergio and Osvaldo she noticed a book of poetry on my desk. I had bought it earlier in the day at a used-book stand in Managua's big outdoor market. The author was Pablo Antonio Cuadra, an important Nicaraguan writer who had fallen out with the revolution and gone into exile.

"Please put away the book," she said. No one had ever told me to put away a book. She saw my confusion and said, "Cuadra is a counterrevolutionary." "I'm sorry," I replied, "but I had no idea that he was a counterrevolutionary. I've never even heard of him. And who cares, anyway? It's only a book of poems." "Just put away the book," she said more firmly this time. She stared at me until I gave in and put the book in my desk drawer.

Sergio laughed when she left the office. "Don't worry about it," he said. "Believe me, nobody cares what you read. She's a good person but not too bright. And she takes her job seriously. She's very Sandinista."

She was in a better mood when she found me in the library some two or three weeks after my encounter with the Sandalistas. "I'd like to speak with you," she said. I followed her into the empty conference room next door. All in one motion she stopped, wheeled around, and said, with the severity of a party bureaucrat, "Your compañeros respect the work you've done so far. And they seem to trust you, politically speaking. Based on their recommendations, the director wants you to work full time with pay at the Center. When you finish your study of the harvesters, the director will find other work for you."

Just like that she had offered me the best job I could have hoped for in Nicaragua. And she stood there waiting for my answer.

I knew at once that I didn't want the job. But after three or four seconds of uneasy silence I asked for time to think about it. She looked irritated but gave me until the end of the week to decide.

There was nothing to think about and nothing to decide. I could not have said why I didn't want the job; I just knew that I didn't want it. I had asked for time only to delay the terrible moment of giving her my decision, which would give the lie to Osvaldo's inscription—"To an American revolutionary"— and cut me off from the Center and the revolution.

I never missed appointments or deadlines, but I missed hers—by a week. And when I finally went to the Center, I went hoping that she wouldn't be there. But she was.

I was alone at my desk when she came into the office. "So, what is your decision?" she asked. I looked away for a few seconds before gathering the courage to meet her eyes and give her the answer that I hadn't even allowed myself to think about: "Thank you, but I can't accept the job."

She looked surprised, hurt, and angry. Clearly she had expected me to accept it. She probably figured that I had asked for time simply to make arrangements back home. And missing her deadline meant nothing. Nobody met deadlines in Nicaragua.

Her stabbing eyes made me both want to apologize as though I had done something wrong and to explain myself even though I had no explanation. After what felt like an excruciatingly long silence, she finally turned on her heels and walked out.

My first thought was, "What if they don't let me stay long enough to finish the study?" I imagined myself going back to school without enough information for my master's thesis. "But of course they'll let me finish the study," I said to myself. "They're reasonable people. And they want the results of my research. Besides, I have a resident visa. What are they going to do, kick me out of the country tomorrow?"

But it was too late. I had just admitted that I cared as much about doing social science for my thesis as I cared about doing social science for the revolution—an admission that burst another of the remaining balloons floating my sinking fantasy of being an American revolutionary.

30

"I'm sorry," said the receptionist. "You can't go into the office wing any more. But you can still use the library and sit in the conference room." She smiled sympathetically as I tried to hide my discomfort at learning that I had lost my desk during lunch.

I hit my low point in Nicaragua while sitting in the conference room and worrying that someone would walk through on their way to the library and see me as a fly-by-night sympathizer. I had always felt superior to the American doctoral students and professors who came to Nicaragua for a few weeks and sat in the conference room copying out information from Sandinista reports on the agrarian reform. They are writing *about* the revolution, I always told myself, while I am writing *for* the revolution. The distinction now seemed marginal at best.

I had been sitting there for ten or fifteen minutes when Sergio and Osvaldo came in. Sergio said he was hoping I would take the job. Osvaldo said he was sorry to see me go. Neither of them seemed angry or resentful. But you are either in or out of a revolutionary transition to socialism. And I had just opted out. So even though I would not be leaving Nicaragua for a couple of months, Sergio and Osvaldo shook my hand—as though they would never see me again.

31

The mosquitoes had vanished along with the rains, but that night I was visited by another disrupter of sleep in the capital city: a big, greasy, winged cockroach. This one was crawling across my bare chest. All at once I woke up, violently flicked the thing away, and shuddered in disgust.

While falling back to sleep, I was visited by an even scarier intruder. For just a second I had a clear image of the fear that haunted me from the back of my mind at the coffee farm—the fear that any differences between me and the Sandalistas were matters of degree rather than kind: that I was more Sandalista than Sandinista.

32

Three or four weeks later I came upon two dogs fighting over a gooey, glistening, reddish-blue piece of highly elastic material. I didn't realize they were pulling and tearing at opposite ends of a placenta until I saw a cow licking a newborn calf under a nearby tree. Ten or fifteen yards beyond the dogs, a naked little boy was playing with an empty Coke bottle on the hard-packed dirt in front of a wooden shack. A thin, middle-aged woman with long, gray hair was wearing a pale-blue sundress and smoking a cigarette in the open doorway. She smiled—salaciously, I thought—when I noticed her looking at me. It felt like I was in a scene from García Márquez's *One Hundred Years of Solitude*, but I was merely on the edge of a miserable village near the cotton fields of Masaya.

Each of its twenty or thirty wooden shacks had a dirt floor and a tin roof. Chickens pecked at bugs under the citrus and mango trees while a pig rooted around a big mound of communal garbage. A light wind carried the smell of pesticides from the cotton fields. Most of the households rented or owned a tiny plot of land on which to grow corn and beans. They all sent two or three family members to pick cotton between December and February.

I walked into the village and saw three men sitting at a picnic table under a cluster of trees next to a dry streambed. One of them called to me to come over. They looked to be in their forties and were wearing short-sleeved shirts and cheap polyester pants. The rubber soles of their leather sandals were made from discarded car tires. A tall, unmarked bottle stood on the table. It was half-filled with clear liquid. Next to the bottle were a jackknife, a shot glass, and a bowl of lemons.

They immediately offered me a glass of *aguardiente*, a high-proof cane liquor. It was barely noon, but they had been drinking for a while. And I could not refuse without causing offense or seeming unmanly. One of the men cut me a slice of lemon and filled the glass. I drank down the aguardiente but sucked too late on the lemon. All at once I shuddered and patted my chest and felt my throat burn. They laughed. It took me a few seconds to compose myself enough to laugh with them.

They each then drank a glass—merely exhaling a soft "ahhh"—before pouring me another. I was quicker with the lemon this time, but I still shivered as the stuff went down. Already I felt a glow.

Only then did they ask who I was. Usually I introduced myself to strangers as a tourist. But I was in their village to interview cotton pickers, so I had to tell them that I was doing a study for the Agrarian Reform Ministry. In addition to mapping out the region's fourteen thousand coffee and cotton harvesters, I was trying to understand what we called the "household division of labor," jargon for what the various members of a family do for work. Few harvesters worked Sundays, so I spent almost every Sunday in a different village interviewing fifteen or twenty cotton or coffee pickers. I asked them whether they owned or rented land, how many people in their family picked coffee or cotton, and what other kinds of work they did.

The man sitting directly across from me turned surly when he heard me say that I was working for the Sandinistas. "They're communists," he said. "I'm just a poor campesino, but I'll never take land from communists. I won't work on their co-operatives or collectives, either. They come around here telling us how to think and what to do. I don't like it."

He paused for a few seconds, which only gave him time

to get madder. "You're an American. You're from the great United States. How can you work for the Sandinistas? I've seen Cubans here, you know. So tell me, how can you work for them?"

His watery eyes boiled with anger, so I kept quiet and hoped he would simmer down. But he slapped the table and said, "I want to know: How can an American work for communists?" He folded his arms tightly across his chest and stared at me. When I didn't answer, he accused me of helping "the traitors of Nicaragua." He even said that it wouldn't be safe for me to interview people in the village. When he looked away and began muttering things I couldn't understand, the man sitting next to him put a hand on his shoulder and told him to take it easy. "He's just a young American who means no harm," he said to his friend. Then he looked at me and said, "You better move along."

My only thought after getting safely out of the village was that a drunk and ornery peasant had prevented me from doing my interviews. I didn't try to excuse his hatred of the Sandinistas, while I surely would have done so a month earlier. Nor did I feel like I was putting my nose in other people's business, as I did after arguing about Trotsky and talking to the coffee farmer.

Turning down the job made me take a step back from the revolution. I told Elena, for example, that I was too busy with my study to keep doing vigilance. I used the same excuse to quit reading the *Primer on Marxism* with the young Sandinistas. I rarely went to the Center and then only to see Sergio and Osvaldo. Some days I didn't even read *Barricada*. And even though I still wanted to believe in the ideal of making socialism in Nicaragua, I seldom felt the inspiring pangs of revolutionary hope and power that I had so often experienced when getting a glimpse of the huge letters "FSLN" atop a big hill in Managua or walking past a new primary school in a shantytown or reading a *Barricada* story about Sandinista soldiers wiping out a base camp of contras.

I had stepped back from the revolution by throwing myself wholly into my study; it had become, in large measure, a means of redemption. An excellent study would fulfill my obligation to the Sandinistas and let me leave Nicaragua on good terms. It would ease my guilt about caring more for my thesis than for the revolution. And it would prove that I was, in the end, more than just a glorified Sandalista.

33

I presented my study in the conference room at the Center a week before leaving Nicaragua. It consisted of several charts and maps, a dozen tables, and thirty handwritten pages of analysis. I had an audience of four: Osvaldo and one person each from the ministry's branches in Managua, Masaya, and Carazo. I made a copy for everyone. I had prepared a presentation, but they wanted to read the entire thing together. So they took turns reading it aloud. Everyone made comments and asked questions along the way.

They liked it. One of them kept saying, "Sí, esto es muy importante" (Yes, this is an important point), while chewing on his cigar and vigorously underlining phrases and circling numbers. Another was impressed by what he called my "theoretical rigor," by which he meant my knowledge of the Marxist literature on the plight of peasants under capitalism. The third praised me for gathering a lot of information in so little time. He especially liked the interview sheets I designed to get economic data on two hundred peasant families.

Osvaldo ended the meeting by saying, "Thank you, Miguel. This is an excellent study. It's too bad," he added with a reproachful smile, "that you're not staying to do more."

After everyone had praised my work and shaken my hand and said they were sorry to see me go, I suddenly wondered, while sitting alone in the conference room, "Where would my study go? Who would use it? For what, if anything? Would I ever know?"

But I didn't really care. All I cared about was having done

Michael Johns

what I set out to do: social science for the revolution. I did
the study that the Frente asked me to do. I did it for free. And
I did it well. My mind was already turning my entire experience of Nicaragua into that one, small, shining story.

Manuel answered his door, gave me a hug, and told me to take a seat at the wrought-iron table in his front patio, which was surrounded by tall plants that smelled sweet and citrusy in the warm evenings. That's how Manuel always greeted me. I had been seeing him every few weeks for five or six months. We met late one night while I was walking home and he was sitting out doing revolutionary vigilance.

Manuel came out a few minutes later with a pack of cigarettes and two cups of black coffee. As always, he lit up as soon as he sat down. Immediately after lighting his first of many cigarettes, he would invariably launch into an analysis of international politics. He sometimes wrote editorials about world affairs for *El Nuevo Diario*, the other pro-Sandinista newspaper. Manuel ended each of our evenings by reading aloud two or three poems by Rubén Darío, Nicaragua's great poet.

On this particular evening, however, our last, I broke his routine by telling him while he lit his first cigarette that I had finished my study and would be leaving Nicaragua in a few days. Manuel did not know that I had turned down the job, so he could not have anticipated the news of my departure. Yet he didn't seem surprised. Nor did he ask why I was leaving.

But he did tell me something that I had never heard before—from him or anyone else. "Nicaragua's revolution will never be as good as Cuba's," he began. "The big island has boxers, dancers, and baseball players who compete at the highest levels. Yes, Cuba restricts political freedoms and individual rights, but it also makes sure that everyone is literate, healthy, and employed. It's also true that Cuba meddles in the affairs of other countries, but it also sends doctors and agronomists to poor socialist countries in Africa and Latin America. And it always goes toe-to-toe with the United States. No thinking person can help but admire Castro because Cuba shows that, in at least some ways, socialism can be as good as capitalism."

He went on to observe that "not one of Nicaragua's comandantes is as talented as Castro. Nor are we Nicaraguans as educated or as cultured as the Cubans were at the start of their revolution. And Managua is a cow town compared to Havana. Nevertheless, our revolution is our best chance to make something of Nicaragua. So I have to try to believe in it, to absorb its promise, to hope that it does more good than harm."

Manuel was the only Nicaraguan I knew who had a mature view of the revolution—perhaps because he was the only adult I knew in Nicaragua. He was twice my age and had a son in the Sandinista army. He even wore the uniform of the middle-aged Latin American intellectual: a guayabera shirt, cotton slacks, and green-tinted glasses in thick, black frames. Everyone else I knew in Nicaragua was in their twenties or early thirties. And they were far too certain about their political beliefs to have enough skepticism for a detached view of life. So it was strange and unsettling to hear a supporter of the revolution say something as tepid as "in at least some ways, socialism can be as good as capitalism," or as tentative as "our revolution is our best chance to make something of Nicaragua. So I have to try to believe in it."

Although I couldn't quite understand Manuel's point of view, it seemed wise to me. And it seemed as though Manuel was treating me as an equal or at least inviting me to come up to his intellectual level. I even had an inkling that my present view of the world might not be my future view of the world.

I had my first inkling, in other words, that I could change my mind about something as fundamental to the Marxian scheme as the idea that capitalism was bad and socialism was good. To admit even the possibility of changing my mind about such a fundamental idea was to take the first step in doing so.

Sergio, Osvaldo, and two or three other people from the ministry gave me a farewell lunch the day before I left Nicaragua. We ate at Managua's only McDonald's. Because the owner had not had anything to do with Somoza, the Frente left his place alone. And because it had become an accepted part of the new Nicaragua, it didn't serve as a symbol of imperialism. In fact, a lot of Sandinistas ate there.

But Managua's McDonald's barely resembled the McDonald's I knew back home—and not only because two AK-47s were leaning against a wall behind the counter. I watched a worker cut a thick slice from a huge block of white cheese and slap it on my hamburger. There were no pickles for the burgers, he said, because they had not gotten their shipment of Bulgarian pickles. He put the burger on waxy brown paper that did not absorb a drop of grease and would not stay wrapped. Instead of Coca-Cola, because they had none, he offered me a fruit drink. And in place of french fries—they had not gotten their shipment of Bulgarian potatoes, either—I got fried cassava.

We took our food and sat outside at a concrete picnic table. Sergio raised his fruit drink and made what was, by all appearances, a friendly joke. "Well Miguel, let's see what you did here in Nicaragua. You read everything we have in the library, you did a brilliant little study that will get lost in a filing cabinet, and you slept with a couple of Nicaraguan girls. Now that's all well and good, but you sure as hell didn't do anything for the revolution!"

I laughed with everyone else, but I knew deep down that his words were as true as they were funny. And I knew that he knew it too.

I came upon a small noontime gathering in front of the student union building in Madison. Thirty or forty students were waiting to hear from a young man in a blue suit who was arranging his notes at a podium. I recognized a thirty-year-old graduate student at the rear of the crowd. He was a self-described anarchist who charged for single bottles of beer at his house parties and loaded his refrigerator with surplus Wisconsin cheese that was distributed free of charge to poor people. When I saw him remove a ripe peach from a small paper bag, I smiled at the thought that he had gotten his fruit from the "free" table at the local food co-op.

He welcomed me back from Nicaragua and told me that a College Republican had just introduced the speaker as a medical student who was studying in Grenada when the United States invaded. We smirked with the knowledge that he was about to peddle the lies of an administration that had just been caught planting mines in Nicaragua's harbors.

The speaker had barely finished his opening line, "I want to thank President Reagan for saving American lives from communist aggression in Grenada," when I grabbed a peach from the anarchist's paper bag and threw it. The peach hit the top corner of the podium and flecked the startled speaker with bits of moist fruit. Someone called me an asshole. And I felt like one. So I walked away hoping that my fellow graduate student, who probably admired what I did, would not tell anyone about it.

The next evening I went to a meeting of Madison's Central American Solidarity Committee, a group that arranged talks in support of the Sandinistas and conducted letter-writing campaigns to congressional representatives who might be sympathetic to cutting off American support for the contras. I went to the meeting to offer my services as a public speaker—and to be admired for working with the Sandinistas. I wanted also to be admired for being a deep thinker who read the heavy stuff. Right before going into the meeting, I actually removed from a paper bag the books I had bought earlier in the day: *Considerations on Western Marxism, Imperialism and Unequal Development*, and *Alienation: Marx's Conception of Man in Capitalist Society*. I put the books in plain view on the table where my fellow activists could be impressed by them.

Two or three days later a graduate student in my department watched me remove a photographic slide from the pencil trough in the top drawer of my desk. He still remembers it. "The memory is vivid," he says, "because I knew at the time there was some curious psychological voodoo surrounding that image. You wanted to show it to me yet you didn't want me to think that you thought it was impressive in any way. So you made jokes about it, dismissed it as absurd, etc., but it was clear to me *then* that you *were* impressed by it."

The photo did indeed hold a curious spell over me. For I liked the image of myself with the AK-47, and I wanted to believe it illustrated my time in Nicaragua, yet I knew that I was not the revolutionary it made me out to be.

Toward the end of my first week back someone gave me a *Harper's* article by V. S. Naipaul about the invasion of Grenada. In the first section of his essay Naipaul reduced the entire affair to this: "In Grenada—133 square miles, 110,000 people—the revolution was as much an imposition—as theatrical and out of scale—as the American military presence it had called up."

Normally I would have dismissed such an equal allocation of blame as flippant and wholly unfair to the victim. But I kept reading. And as hard as I tried, I could not dismiss Naipaul's general depiction of the revolution as a farce. I didn't

even mind his mocking an American sympathizer who wrote
this poem about Grenada's revolution:

> *de forest move*
> *de land watch*
> *de folk talk.*
> *de cat mew*
> *de dog bark*
> *de revo start.*

I shared the poem with the graduate student who saw the
photo of me with the rifle. For several days afterward I said
"de dog bark" and he replied "de revo start" when we passed
each other in the hallways.

All in one week, I had somehow managed to throw a peach
at an apologist for Reagan's invasion of Grenada while seeing the truth in Naipaul's depiction of its revolution; to show
off as a deep-thinking Marxist while sensing the voodoo in
the photograph of me as a revolutionary; and to feel uneasy
while giving the first of a dozen talks over several months in
support of the Sandinistas.

I felt uneasy giving the talk because I wasn't sure what to
say. Most American sympathizers were not Marxists, so it
was unwise to tell them that the Frente was a vanguard party
trying to build socialism in Nicaragua. Besides, I was starting
to have some embryonic doubts about socialism myself.

So I peddled the Frente's lines about a mixed economy,
political pluralism, and international nonalignment, though
I knew they were simplistic and misleading. I even gave advance praise for the upcoming election of November 1984,
though I knew full well that the Frente saw the election as
a political concession rather than a political principle. The
Frente wanted to build a socialist society, after all, not an
electoral democracy. And losing an election would mean losing the revolution. The only thing I said with conviction—
and without facts—was that the contras were nothing but
CIA puppets who were paid to destroy the revolution.

It took me four or five talks to realize that I was giving my church-basement audiences in Madison and Milwaukee the same half-truths that the young Sandinista had given his Sandalista audience in Managua. From then on, every talk got harder to give. They began to feel more like a duty than a pleasure. And with each passing week I drifted further from the revolution—and not only because I was no longer in Nicaragua. I never wrote to Sergio or Osvaldo or Soraya. I didn't read the international edition of *Barricada*, which was available at a leftist bookstore in Madison. I felt less and less like the valiant American who had just come back from working with the Sandinistas. Even as I began to turn my research for the revolution into a thesis for my master's degree, I saw Nicaragua's cotton and coffee harvests as numbers, as abstractions, as flows on a map that might have been anywhere in Central America.

At some point I began making excuses for why I could not give talks or attend meetings of the solidarity committee. I even stopped going to the weekly house parties that were hosted by Latin American students and filled with the sounds of Spanish, the revolutionary music of Silvio Rodríguez, and heated discussions about Nicaragua, El Salvador, and American imperialism. Yet I never acknowledged that I was letting go of the Sandinistas. And despite some moments of guilt, like the time I broke my promise to send the director of the Center a Spanish translation of my thesis, the revolution sank quietly to the bottom of my mind, where it got buried as an unexamined memory.

37

Had I taken the job with the Center, I almost certainly would have gotten my political comeuppance within a few months. But I returned to graduate school, where it took me a few years—*after* giving my last talk about the Sandinistas—to start letting go of the Marxism that inspired their revolution.

It took me a few years because it was easy to revert to academic Marxism after failing at revolutionary Marxism. Reverting was easy because once I left the reality of a socialist revolution for the shelter of an American university, there was no pressure to think realistically about the revolution, my experience of it, or the ideas behind it.

And I still liked the ideas, of which I got plenty at the Johns Hopkins University, where I got my Ph.D. under the guidance of a very smart Marxist geographer. I still liked the ideas because I still wanted a big view of the world and the feeling of intellectual power and control that goes with it. Moreover, I had yet to outgrow the radical identity that comes from seeing capitalism as the problem. Orwell was barely exaggerating when he said in his essay "Writers and Leviathan" that the "whole left-wing ideology" is "utterly contemptuous of . . . governments, laws, prisons, police forces, armies, flags, frontiers, patriotism, religion, conventional morality, and, in fact, the whole existing scheme of things." My political and intellectual identity had been built on exactly that kind of contempt, and it was not easy letting go of the feeling of superiority that went with it.

Like the base of a seaside cliff, however, the foundation to my faith in Marxism was steadily eroding. The process was almost too slow to notice, but the more I learned about life the less the categories of Marxism made sense of it. Sometimes I even wondered whether using the Marxian categories was merely engaging in an intellectual version of painting by numbers—instead of thinking for oneself. With each passing month, I lost a bit of the intellectual and political certainty that Marxism is so good at providing. And the more I learned to accept the uncertainties of life, the less contempt I felt for "the whole existing scheme of things."

38

In February 1990 the Frente got trounced in a national election. Before handing the powers of government to the winning party, the Frente handed itself large pieces of the property it had confiscated in the name of the revolution. Many of the Frente's top men did worse than that: they turned the property of the people into their very own *private* property—private property that would help them make the transition from big-time revolutionaries to big-time businessmen, politicians, and influence peddlers. Nicaraguans called the giveaway *la piñata,* after the birthday game in which blindfolded kids swing a stick to bust open a papier-mâché animal filled with goodies.

I was far too removed from Nicaragua to care that the Frente lost the election—and its revolution. I wasn't even surprised to learn that several comandantes had played piñata with their country's wealth. And I had come to believe, while writing my dissertation about the economy and culture of Buenos Aires in the late nineteenth century, that Marxism was simply too big, abstract, and tendentious to say very much that was meaningful about particular places and people.

I was rejecting exactly that which had drawn me to Marxism in the first place: the idea that you can know enough about human society to fix its problems. At some point I literally said to myself, "Even the smartest, kindest, and most level-headed person is lucky to know the half of what he or she is doing even half of the time—never mind what everyone else is doing." Despite my growing appreciation for the complexity of life, I had yet to fully come to grips with the Sandinista revolution or the prospects for socialism.

My moment of truth came a few months after the Frente lost the election. The revolution was officially over, the piñata had exposed the inner rot of the Sandinistas, and late one night while packing my stuff for Berkeley, California, where I was about to start my job as a professor, I found a box that I had not opened since finishing my master's thesis some five years before. I sat on the floor and looked through my material from Nicaragua.

Among a folder of *Barricada* clippings was an editorial that Osvaldo had brought to the office one day. He had underlined two phrases that he wanted to discuss with me and Sergio: "The workers must take over the productive forces and means of production to create the new society" and "The economic, political, and administrative management of the country ought to be taken increasingly out of the hands of professionals and bureaucrats and put into those of the working masses."

Of course we agreed that the working masses should eventually take over the means of production and fulfill their historical destiny of making socialism. We even agreed that the masses should begin taking over sooner rather than later.

But I could now see that we never really believed it. We were supposed to believe it. We wanted to believe it. And we certainly would have felt guilty and confused if we had not believed it. But each of us, it now seemed to me, had secret doubts about the masses ever taking over.

And the more I thought about it, the more the idea of Sandinistas like Sergio and Osvaldo—never mind the Center's director or the Frente's comandantes—ever ceding power to the working masses seemed, well, preposterous. Even more preposterous was the idea of the working masses collectively running the farms, the factories, and the various ministries of government.

I then found a speech in which one of the comandantes said the Frente had no intention of turning Nicaragua into "just another Costa Rica." While bourgeois Costa Rica gives its left political freedom, said the comandante, revolutionary Nicaragua was giving its left political power—the power to turn Nicaragua into a socialist society.

The very idea that drove me to Nicaragua now looked like a fatal mistake. If only the Frente, I thought to myself, would have tried by some weird twist of fate to do precisely what the comandante said it would never do: turn Nicaragua into "just another Costa Rica."

I had not swapped my Marxist utopia for a liberal one. I knew too well the odds against turning a violent and disorderly nation like Nicaragua into a stable and well-organized capitalist democracy like Costa Rica, which abolished its army in 1948 and was better off in every way than the rest of Central America. But I also knew that catching up to capitalist Costa Rica had at least a small chance of success, while chasing socialism, I said to myself, was nothing more than chasing a chimera.

A second later the insight came fully into view. It's a chimera, I told myself, because man is simply man. There is no new man. And without a new man there is no new society. I laughed at myself because I knew that my father, who had never stepped foot on a college campus, could have told me as much the day I went to Nicaragua.

39

For the next sixteen or seventeen years I rarely talked about my time in Nicaragua. And when I did I explained it either by saying that Marx's ideas were too enticing not to act on them or by resorting to the old cliché "If you're not a communist at twenty you have no heart; if you're not an anticommunist at thirty you have no brain." Both lines had an element of truth, but they were mere lines. They made me feel good about getting into Marxism and better for getting out, and they kept me from having to think honestly about why I went to Nicaragua and what happened to me while I was there.

Not until I saw my younger self in a seminar full of radical graduate students did I fully realize that I had never truly believed in Marxism—if only because I had never truly thought about it. The only way to believe in such a grandiose view of life, after all, is by not thinking about it.

Most of the nine or ten students in the seminar were working with a group of Marxist professors who dominated our department. For some fifteen years I had gotten along with my Marxist colleagues by avoiding all discussions of ideas and politics. But I failed to get along with their young protégés, whose ideas and political opinions I had to hear every week in a seminar that I taught for our incoming graduate students.

They shared an approach: accentuate the injustices in life; take righteous umbrage at every incident that can be construed (or misconstrued) as racist, sexist, classist, colonial-

ist, imperialist, or ethnocentric; and blame it all on capitalism. They took the same approach, in other words, that I had
taken as a first-year graduate student some twenty-five years
before.

Just a few weeks into the seminar one student brashly
said, "The problem with you, Professor Johns, is that you're
an apologist for capitalism." I had earned his scorn by saying
that it made no sense to blame our ills on something as big
and as old and as varied as capitalism, which in and of itself
explains next to nothing about anything.

Halfway through the class two students asked me to
change the rest of the syllabus. "It doesn't speak to us," one
of them said. They wanted more "critical theory," a euphemism for various strains of neo-Marxism. They were getting
plenty of critical theory in their other classes, but all they
wanted was more of what they thought they already knew.

They didn't like me saying that critical theory was no better than any other form of social thought or that they—as
graduate students who were being paid to think—had an intellectual duty to think as critically about critical theory as
they thought about every other social science theory. They
liked it even less when I asked a question that I too would
have resented at their age: whether they liked Marxism
(and critical theory) not simply because they thought it was
"right," but because their professors liked it or because they
saw it as a path to academic success or because it reinforced
their political opinions and their images of themselves as
radical students.

Desperate to keep their waning attention, I tried to earn
some political respect by telling them about my research
for the Sandinistas. That I had worked for a revolutionary
government at their age did nothing, however, to stop them
from dismissing my ideas. And when I used the example of
Nicaragua's revolution to point out the dishonesty of blam-
ing our ills on capitalism when we can't even imagine a realistic and worthy kind of socialism, one student accused me of

Michael Johns

"closing off the possibilities for political liberation." Another countered my skepticism with a favorite phrase of Marxists: "pessimism of the intelligence, optimism of the will." I lost the students for good when I asked, rhetorically, "Isn't that just a clever way of saying, 'Those may be the facts, but that's not how I feel?'"

40

Near the end of the semester one of the graduate students was in my office telling me about his plan for writing a seminar paper on Marxist theories of underdevelopment. Suddenly I wasn't hearing him. I wasn't even seeing him. I was looking right through him, as it were, and into myself at his age—exactly what I had been afraid of seeing all semester long. I saw myself as a radish. After twenty-five years of forgetting, I finally remembered Enrique's calling me a rábano. And I finally understood that I was never truly a revolutionary, a radical, or even a Marxist. All I had ever been was a radish.

EPILOGUE

If Trotsky and Che went to their graves believing in world socialism and Castro goes to his believing in Cuban communism, most revolutionaries go to theirs knowing that they have been radishes. Every one of the Frente's comandantes, for example, gave up the idea of creating the new man in Nicaragua. In fact, most of them ended their revolutionary careers by playing the role of Napoleon in Orwell's *Animal Farm*. Just as the revolutionary pig betrayed his fellow farm animals by joining their human oppressors, so did most of the Frente's leaders abandon the workers and peasants to join the very class of capitalists that their revolution had set out to destroy.

Plenty of Marxists stay red to the end, but the die-hards tend to be academics rather than revolutionaries. There have always been many more devout, happy, and middle-aged Marxists in American universities than in all of the former Soviet Union and its communist allies put together—precisely because academics rarely, if ever, see Marxism in action. And when they do, it's as visitors to someone else's revolution.

Sociologist Paul Hollander calls such visitors "Political Pilgrims," the title of his book about the tens of thousands of "Western intellectuals" who supported, traveled to, and sometimes worked for young socialist regimes in the Soviet Union, China, and Cuba. Thousands more lined up behind Chile's socialists, Nicaragua's Sandinistas, and Mexico's Zapatista rebels.

But no matter how hard you fall for someone else's revolution, you never commit to it. Nor do you take responsibility for it. You certainly don't have to worry about living with its consequences. Whether you show your sympathy by marching on campus, picking coffee on a collective farm, or doing a study for an Agrarian Reform Ministry, you always know, deep down, anyway, that it is not your revolution or your country or your future.

This unavoidable distance softens the reality of revolution and makes it easy for socialist sympathizers to hold on indefinitely to the utopian outlook and the oppositional attitude that lie at the core of Marxism. In his book *Capitalism, Socialism, and Democracy*, the economist Joseph Schumpeter explains the logic, as it were, of Marxism's core traits. "In one important sense," writes Schumpeter, "Marxism *is* a religion. To the believer it presents, first, a system of ultimate ends that embody the meaning of life and are absolute standards by which to judge events and actions; and, secondly, a guide to those ends which implies a plan of salvation and the indication of the evil from which mankind, or a chosen section of mankind, is to be saved."

Once you adopt absolute rather than realistic standards for judging human affairs—once you believe that humans are capable of reaching near-perfect states of justice, harmony, equality, fulfillment, and liberation—you thereby commit yourself to seeing even the finest liberal democracy as a failure. And once you blame the failings of liberal democracy on the evil of capitalism rather than on the frailties of human beings, you have no choice but to see socialism as the solution.

But no one opposes capitalism on intellectual grounds alone. One's politics, after all, are an extension of one's character. Believing in something as fantastical as full-on socialism—especially if you live in the United States—is as much "an emanation of an inner dissatisfaction," says Eric Hoffer in *The Passionate Mind*, as it is a "response to stimuli from without." A need to feel right or virtuous or contrarian, in other words, or to feel a sense of hope or salvation in some grand but secular purpose, is as important as the perceived injustice of capitalism itself in driving someone to the far left.

The utopian and oppositional core of Marxism burns hottest in Third World revolutionaries, but it burns longest in Western intellectuals. Marxists are actually at their very best in First World universities. There they have no power to do anything but criticize. They face no pressure to be realistic about their ideas. Their political action consists almost entirely of signing petitions, giving talks on campus, taping protest posters to their office doors, getting more leftists into their departments, and, if they're lucky, taking a pilgrimage to a socialist revolution—where, says Hollander, they look for "glorious alternatives to their own flawed society."

Because American Marxism is merely another school of thought in the social sciences, it serves mainly as a means to academic success. And because Marxism hardly matters in American politics, it affords its followers a gratifying identity. It is the identity of the self-described critical thinker who knows better than everyone else and sees himself as part of a put-upon intellectual minority that, as a Marxist colleague of mine liked to say, "speaks truth to the powers of capitalism." He never mentioned the key to his identity: the powers of capitalism were not listening.

We expect intellectuals to think honestly and curb their prejudices, but they are no better than anyone else at facing uncomfortable facts—especially facts that make them uncomfortable about their politics. Political beliefs are highly subjective to begin with, but the more radical they are the more certainty they need, and the more certainty they need the fewer facts they can handle.

In order to believe, for example, that capitalism causes our problems and socialism can solve them, you must blind yourself to the huge mass of facts that suggest we humans are innately flawed creatures who will never fully understand our faults—never mind fix them. For five, ten, perhaps fifteen years, the sheer hope and audacity of trying to make the new man can blind the young revolutionary to the impossibility of his task. But the facts of life eventually overwhelm his theories. The academic, on the other hand, enjoys enough distance from the facts of socialism to retain his ideal of it—and the radical identity that goes with it.

I recently had a version of a conversation that I have had dozens of times over the past twenty years. A middle-aged professor was telling me about her new class, "The Final Crisis of Capitalism?" The question mark was a sign of her hope.

"Have you ever imagined what full-on socialism would actually look like?" I asked her. "That is, can you actually imagine, in concrete terms, real human beings acting like new socialist beings in their new society?"

Without blinking she said, "No, I can't. But I don't have to. Humans are utterly flexible. Every culture is different. The possible combinations are endless. History is all about change. So why worry about human limits and shut down our possibilities for liberation? I have no doubt that we can make ourselves into something we can't yet perceive because, as I said, we've already changed so much and, more to the point, there is far too little 'human nature'"—she made quotation marks with her fingers—"to limit that which we can become, which, as far as I'm concerned, is anything we want to become."

"But what have you learned from your study of human history," I asked her, "or from your personal life and the times you've lived in, or from the latest work in evolutionary biology and the science of the mind, that gives you the idea that we humans can somehow escape our evolutionary past and become some sort of harmonious and egalitarian beings we've never seen before? And all by creating the 'correct' economic and social conditions"—now it was my turn to finger the quotation marks—"and by putting the 'correct' ideas in people's heads? Besides, don't you think that cultures have many more commonalities than differences, and that every culture is just a riff on universal human features?"

"Your belief," she said, "that there truly is a human nature and that it is incompatible with a full-throated and fully liberated socialism is purely ideological. In fact, it is nothing more than a fiction that serves the interests of capitalism."

"The real fiction," I replied, "is your line of reasoning, which has nothing to do with the facts of life and everything to do with providing intellectual cover for your political fantasy."

Had our conversation continued, she would have had an equally hard time dealing with another set of facts: those about real-life socialism. In their books *Political Pilgrims: Travels of Western Intellectuals to the Soviet Union, China, and Cuba* and *Past Imperfect: French Intellectuals, 1944–1956*, Paul Hollander and Tony Judt document a consistent pattern. While radical intellectuals show an acute sensitivity to social injustices and abuses of power in their own countries, they ignore injustices and abuses in socialist countries. And when they can't ignore them, they explain them away. It is not, they say, the internal contradictions of socialism that cause it to fail, but external factors like imperialist aggression or elitist vanguards or heavy bureaucracies or economic backwardness or a lack of time.

Like George Orwell and Charles Darwin, the sociologist Max Weber understood the need to face uncomfortable and unfavorable facts. He also understood how hard it is. "The primary task of a useful teacher," he says in his essay "Science as a Vocation," "is to teach his students to recognize 'inconvenient' facts—I mean facts that are inconvenient for their party opinions. . . . I believe the teacher accomplishes more than a mere intellectual task if he compels his audience to accustom itself to the existence of such facts. I would be so immodest as even to apply the expression 'moral achievement,' though perhaps this may sound too grandiose for something that should go without saying."